SHOP LONDON

AN INSIDER'S GUIDE TO SPENDING LIKE A LOCAL

EMMA MCCARTHY

PHOTOGRAPHS BY KIM LIGHTBODY

FRANCES
LINCOLN

CONTENTS

INTRODUCTION

Want to know where to find a vast collection of vintage Yves Saint Laurent? Or to know where Winston Churchill bought his cigars? Ask a Londoner. There is no population in the world that's better versed — or better placed — to curate a shopping trip of which dreams are made. The key lies in knowing where to point your feet. If it's a new shopping district that you're after, use the front of this book to locate the very best, often under-the-radar destinations. A far cry from the city's many tourist trap thoroughfares, these are off-the-beaten-track high streets lined with more independent stores than even the most seasoned shopaholic could imagine. Meanwhile, for a detailed directory of the city's shopping genres — from antiques to eco-conscious boutiques — let the second half of this book be your guide. There you will find a list of the very best shops in the city by category, from the top bookshops to where to head for to the chicest Scandi furniture. Whatever your shopping motivation, rest assured that London has it covered.
Comfy shoes are essential.

RUSSELL SQUARE

GREAT ORMOND STREET

LAMB'S CONDUIT STREET

RUGBY STREET

EMERALD STREET

PERSEPHONE BOOKS

17 PENREATH & HALL 17A

Lamb's Conduit Street

1 FOLK

2 PENREATH & HALL

3 GRENSON

4 PERSEPHONE BOOKS

5 THORNBACK & PEEL

LAMB'S CONDUIT STREET

Tucked away among the back streets of Bloomsbury, this partly
residential street is a favourite with clued-up Londoners.
Its grand Georgian townhouses have long been home to a close-
knit community of homegrown menswear brands including Folk,
Grenson and Oliver Spencer. But it wasn't until US retailer
J Crew moved into the neighbourhood with a dedicated men's store
that Lamb's Conduit Street stopped being such a tightly held
secret and became a fully-fledged shopping destination.
But it's not all about the boys. The patch is also unique when
it comes to tarting up your home. Line your shelves with
historic women's fiction from Persephone Books, spruce up your
bricks and mortar with the help of Pentreath & Hall and fill
your fridge at The People's Supermarket food cooperative.
Also, don't pass up the opportunity for a mid-ramble pint at
The Lamb – said to be a favoured watering hole of past local
residents Sylvia Plath, Ted Hughes and Charles Dickens.

FOLK

Since its conception in 2001 by Scotsman Cathal McAteer, this menswear brand has quietly established itself as a purveyor of unpretentious style. The airy, whitewashed shop displays its signature workman's jackets and chunky ribbed knits in suitably industrial surroundings. The street is also home to the brand's only dedicated women's store at number 53.

---

49 Lamb's Conduit Street, WC1N 3NG.
020 7404 6458
www.folkclothing.com

◀ PENTREATH & HALL

Tucked away down a quiet Georgian street, interior designer Ben Pentreath and artist Bridie Hall's beautiful little shop is filled with treasures for the home which are quintessentially British but far from twee. Great for gifts but equally good for moments of distraction, it is a must-visit for discovering things you never knew you needed.

—

17 Rugby Street, WC1N 3QT.
020 7430 2526
www.pentreath-hall.com

GRENSON

Founded in Northamptonshire in 1866 by Mr William Green, Grenson was one of the first producers in the world to use the Goodyear welting construction method – now a hallmark of all well-made British shoes. But despite its impressive lineage, the brand hasn't lost touch with what the modern man wants from his footwear. Its minimalist flagship shop – the largest of four in London – houses boots and brogues made with the same traditional approach to design but with a distinctively fashion-forward flavour, making them popular with City boys and Shoreditch types alike. In 2011, Grenson expanded its offering to include women's styles too. Its stacked-sole brogues and tasselled loafers remain among the bestsellers.

—

40 Lamb's Conduit Street, WC1N 3LB.
020 3689 2970
www.grenson.com

PERSEPHONE BOOKS

The next time you feel like brushing up on your knowledge of little-known twentieth-century female writers, head straight for Persephone Books. Its picture-postcard storefront conceals a wealth of forgotten works by women, rebound in chic, signature grey covers, decorated with beautiful endpapers, and ready to enjoy the cult following they deserve.

—

59 Lamb's Conduit Street, WC1N 3NB.
020 7242 9292
www.persephonebooks.co.uk

THORNBACK & PEEL

Former florist Juliet Thornback and theatre designer Delia Peel launched their brand in 2007 with the aim of bringing a touch of British humour to the home. Inspired by the legendary Mrs Beeton and Beatrix Potter's Mr McGregor, this quaint shop is filled with a cornucopia of kitchenware splashed with kitsch screen-printed designs, from cabbages and rabbits to Victorian jellies.

———

7 Rugby Street, WC1N 3QT.
020 7831 2878
www.thornbackandpeel.co.uk

FOUR MORE

- **Connock & Lockie**
  A bespoke tailors established in 1902,
  Connock & Lockie specialise in old school
  tailoring excellence with gentlemanly flare.
  33 Lamb's Conduit Street, WC1N 3NG.
  www.connockandlockie.com

- **Universal Works**
  The menswear brand's first standalone store is a
  go-to for guys looking to invest in staple t-shirts,
  trucker jackets and crew neck knits.
  37 Lamb's Conduit Street, WC1N 3NG.
  www.universalworks.co.uk

- **Oliver Spencer**
  Shopping at Oliver Spencer is as relaxed as the
  clothes within it. The store sells scents from
  Margate-based Haeckels and bags by Porter-
  Yoshida & Co alongside its menswear line.
  62 Lamb's Conduit Street, WC1N 3LW.
  www.oliverspencer.co.uk

- **The People's Supermarket**
  Community-minded, ethical grocery store run
  'for the people, by the people' with an emphasis
  on seasonal, locally-sourced produce.
  72-76 Lamb's Conduit Street, WC1N 3LP.
  www.thepeoplessupermarket.org

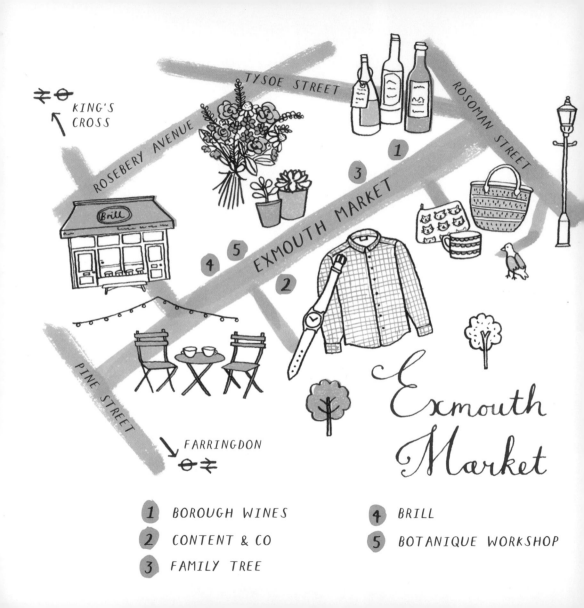

TYSOE STREET

ROSEBERY AVENUE

ROSOMAN STREET

KING'S CROSS

EXMOUTH MARKET

Brill

PINE STREET

FARRINGDON

Exmouth Market

1 BOROUGH WINES
2 CONTENT & CO
3 FAMILY TREE
4 BRILL
5 BOTANIQUE WORKSHOP

EXMOUTH MARKET

The street that was once famous for its London boozers and fruit and veg stalls has been transformed into a foodie destination. And as every Londoner knows, where there are restaurants and bars the retail opportunities are plentiful, so it was only a matter of time before the street piqued the interest of some of the capital's most creative shopkeepers. Start your spree with a caffeine fix at Caravan before stopping to smell the roses at Botanique, pick up a bottle at Borough Wines or a page-turner at Bookends, and finish up with a retro rummage and a sweet treat at the Clerkenwell Vintage Fashion Fair.

◄ BOROUGH WINES

The capital's best-loved bottle shops began life with just 10 organic wines sold at Borough Market. The varieties of plonk now extend to well over 300. Pioneers of the wallet-friendly refillable bottle scheme, this Exmouth outpost (the sixth of the brand's eight branches) has also introduced a self-service growler system for beer guzzlers.

---

63 Exmouth Market, EC1R 4QL.
020 7837 1076
www.boroughwines.co.uk

CONTENT & CO

The younger – and arguably cooler – brother of The Content Store on Lamb's Conduit Street, this men's garb outpost houses a wealth of collaborations with cult labels. Edwin denim, Red Wing boots and fisherman sweaters by Danish brand SNS Herning unite in what makes for one exceptionally stylish capsule wardrobe.

---

30 Exmouth Market, EC1R 4QE.
020 7833 1101
www.contentstorelondon.com

FAMILY TREE

A charming little gift shop big on eco-conscious design. Owner Takako Copeland sources homeware and accessories from across the globe – from handwoven toys from Sri Lanka to felt booties made by fairtrade artisans in Nepal. Closer to home the studio also champions local craftspeople and designs its own original prints and jewellery.

—

53 Exmouth Market, EC1R 4QL.
020 7278 1084
www.familytreeshop.co.uk

BRILL

Brill – part record store, part coffee shop – is a great place to while away a lazy afternoon with a flat white and a bit of Fleetwood Mac. The snug café's menu is loaded with filled Brick Lane bagels and tasty sweet bakes, while its great soundtrack and CD stockpile spans jazz and blues to folk and rock.

—

27 Exmouth Market, EC1R 4QL.
020 7833 9757
www.exmouth.london/brill

BOTANIQUE WORKSHOP

Whether you're after a hand-tied bouquet of blooms or a unique botanical gift fresh off the workbench, owner Alice, florist Pip and crucially, Goose the shop dog are on hand to help. This plant shop specialises in potted succulents and contemporary arrangements – they offer home delivery to most central London postcodes too – while intimate floristry workshops span flower crown and wreath making classes. Botanique also stocks a meticulously curated edit of treasures from local producers including Hackney-based kidswear label What Mother Made and Netil Market's dog-loving brand Fetch and Follow. Add in its charming collection of handmade cards and you've got the perfect pre-party pitstop.

—

31 Exmouth Market, EC1R 4QL.
No phone.
www.botaniqueworkshop.com

FOUR MORE

- **Bookends**
  Alongside an extensive selection of children's titles, Bookends is home to one of the largest origami collections in the UK.
  66 Exmouth Market, EC1R 4QP.
  www.bookendslondon.co.uk

- **Bagman & Robin**
  Catering for those who desire one-of-a-kind arm candy, Bagman & Robin create bags out of rare leather and vintage Japanese kimono fabric.
  47 Exmouth Market, EC1R 4QL.
  www.bagmanandrobin.com

- **Clerkenwell Vintage Fashion Fair**
  A regular vintage market with hordes of garments and trinkets to rummage through. The grand venue also houses a pop-up nail bar and retro tea room. Check the website for the next date.
  The Old Finsbury Town Hall, Rosebery Avenue, EC1R 4RP.
  www.clerkenwellvintagefashionfair.co.uk

- **McCaul Goldsmiths**
  Contemporary fine jewellery atelier with an open workshop. Browse the collections and watch the goldsmiths at work using century-old techniques.
  56 Exmouth Market, EC1R 4QE.
  www.mccaul.com

BAKER STREET

BAKER STREET

CHILTERN STREET

MANCHESTER STREET

TRUNK

BLANDFORD STREET

GEORGE STREET

MONOCLE

Chiltern Street

1   MOUKI MOU

2   CADENHEAD'S WHISKY SHOP & TASTING ROOM

3   CIRE TRUDON

4   TRUNK

5   THE MONOCLE SHOP

CHILTERN STREET

Since the arrival of celebrity dining hangout
Chiltern Firehouse, this NW1 stretch has given neighbouring
Marylebone High Street a run for its money as the shopping
magnet of choice for affluent locals with impeccable taste and
deep pockets. But Chiltern Street's appeal runs deeper than the
chance to spot an A-lister (though that certainly helps).
Men are particularly well catered for: notice the authentic
cool of Trunk and John Simmons. Plus, the area has a stellar
reputation for its specialist boutiques. Cire Trudon's candles
are a must-buy for anyone throwing a posh dinner party while
upmarket holiday shop Prism is a destination all of its own.

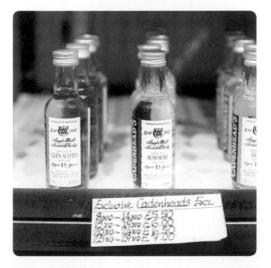

◀ MOUKI MOU

Conceived by fashion showroom agent Maria Lemos, this bijou boutique is a celebration of understated luxury. Discover niche jewellers on the ground floor or descend the spiral staircase into a warren of tiny, tiled rooms that contain a concentration of under-the-radar labels including draped dresses by Dosa and denim by 45rpm.

—

29 Chiltern Street, W1U 7PL.
020 7224 4010
www.moukimou.com

CADENHEAD'S WHISKY SHOP & TASTING ROOM ▶

Scotland's oldest independent whisky bottler relocated to the area from Covent Garden in 2008. Begin your search for the perfect dram in the front room, home to its signature Scottish whiskies, or venture further in to discover international blends and Cadenhead's rums. The shop also offers regular sessions in its two tasting lounges.

—

26 Chiltern Street, W1U 7QF.
020 7935 6999
www.whiskytastingroom.com

◄ CIRE TRUDON

With a history dating back to the 1600s, Paris's Cire Trudon is the oldest and most prestigious candle-maker in the world and counts Louis XIV and Marie Antoinette as historic fans. Its first branch outside France masquerades as an elegant drawing room with ornate wallpaper, bell jars and wax busts. Don't miss the hidden Fornasetti Profumi store out back.

—

36 Chiltern Street, W1U 7QJ.
020 7486 7590
www.trudon.com

TRUNK

Setting up shop in 2010, Trunk's owner Mats Klingberg set a benchmark for one-stop menswear shopping. Its two-storey boutique at number 8 was the first to bring respected international brands such as Beams+, Aspesi and Montedoro to London, while its accessories-focused Labs offshoot at number 34 supplies all the finishing touches.

—

8 Chiltern Street, W1U 7PU.
020 7486 2357
www.trunkclothiers.com

THE MONOCLE SHOP

This bricks and mortar outpost for chic global affairs magazine Monocle was launched in November 2008 as a pop up, but its popularity has seen it stand the test of time. An oasis for the discerning, the shop is filled with the mag's signature Porter bags, plus stylish stationery and knitwear. The excellent Monocle Café is also a stone's throw away on Chiltern Street.

—

2A George Street, W1U 3QS.
020 7486 8770
www.monocle.com

FOUR MORE

- **Prism**
  Former fashion editor Anna Laub's label began life as an opticals brand, before expanding to include sunglasses and super-stylish swimwear. *54 Chiltern Street, W1U 7QX. www.prismlondon.com*

- **The Conran Shop**
  On neighbouring Marylebone High Street, this three-floor Mecca for homeware loveliness is the sort of shop you could easily move into. *55 Marylebone High Street, W1U 5HS. www.theconranshop.co.uk*

- **Daunt Books**
  Literary lovers flock to this iconic Edwardian bookshop (organised geographically) to admire its majestic oak balconies and conservatory roof. *83 Marylebone High Street, W1U 4QW. www.dauntbooks.co.uk*

- **Cabbages & Frocks Market**
  Held in a cobbled churchyard, this Saturday market brings together a fine feast of fashion and food. *St. Marylebone Parish Church Grounds, W1U 5BA. www.cabbagesandfrocks.co.uk*

HIGHBURY & ISLINGTON

BARNSBURY STREET

Upper Street

ARIA

UPPER STREET

CROSS STREET

ESSEX ROAD

CAMDEN PASSAGE

COLEBROOKE ROW

ANGEL

1 GILL WING COOKSHOP

2 ANNIE'S

3 HEXAGONE

4 ARIA

5 TWENTYTWENTYONE

UPPER STREET

It may be nicknamed 'Supper Street' because of its dense
population of restaurants, but this North London artery
– running from Angel tube station to Highbury Corner – has
much to offer the discerning shopper too. Upper Street
is prime real estate for a host of high street boutiques that
have played an integral role in its gentrification, however
it continues to be defined by the independents on which it
was founded. Picturesque offshoot Camden Passage remains a
vanguard of vintage fashion and antiques. Historically, the
area is known for being an epicentre for the radical left and
was once home to Sisterwrite, Britain's first feminist bookshop.
Nowadays, design is the watchword, and there are plenty of
places to kit out a multi-million pound townhouse. Incidentally,
there is no shortage of these in this desirable postcode.

◀ GILL WING COOKSHOP

The trump card in Gill Wing's Upper Street
monopoly (other outposts include stores dedicated
to shoes, jewellery and gifts), this cookshop is
crammed with every kitchen utensil known to man.
Pick your way through the labyrinth of
Le Creuset pots and melon ballers and remember:
if Gill Wing doesn't stock it, it's not worth having
in your kitchen.

—

190 Upper Street, N1 1RQ.
020 7226 5392
www.gillwing.co.uk

ANNIE'S ▶

This North London institution has been trading
in vintage treasures for over 40 years and prides
itself on its stash of original 1920s flapper dresses,
enough to make Daisy Buchanan green with envy.
It's not short of modern-day admirers too – pop in
for a petticoat and you might spot long-time fan
Kate Moss browsing the fur coats next to you.

—

12 Camden Passage, N1 8ED.
020 7359 0796
www.anniesvintageclothing.co.uk

◀ HEXAGONE

A chic celebration of all things French, Hexagone divides its continental collection into six categories – home, fashion, beauty, household, stationery and kids. Highlights include Opinel knives famously used for sculpting by Picasso, riding boots from heritage-listed La Botte Gardiane and Atelier Buffile ceramics selected for their 'je ne sais quoi'.

—

12B Camden Passage, N1 8ED.
0207 288 1444
www.hexagone-uk.com

ARIA

Set in the grand surrounds of Islington's Barnsbury Hall, Aria is possibly the most picturesque place in London to seek home inspiration. After taking in the building's many lovingly restored original features – most impressive of which is the vaulted ceiling on the upper level – there's a bounty of thoroughly modern furniture to browse. Big draws come via contemporary design heavyweights including Arne Jacobson chairs and Alessi kitchenware, which sit alongside the instantly recognisable work of satirical artist David Shrigley. The highly giftable selection of toiletries (Compagnie de Provence, Cowshed) and excellent gift selection are just two more reasons why Aria is a joy to visit. Be sure not to overlook the unique jewellery by homegrown designers.

—

Barnsbury Hall, Barnsbury Street, N1 1PN.
020 7704 6222
www.ariashop.co.uk

TWENTYTWENTYONE

Championing a progressive approach to classic twentieth-century design, twentytwentyone work with over 60 of the world's leading designers for its ever-evolving portfolio. But you don't need to be an expert to appreciate its retro-cool wares. This much-loved design store has also supplied furniture to iconic landmarks including Tate Modern's Switch House and the Mondrian Hotel.

274-275 Upper Street, N1 2UA.
020 7288 1996
www.twentytwentyone.com

FOUR MORE

- **SMUG**
  Graphic designer Lizzie Evans's collection of quirky, homely objects make for a boutique that's thoroughly deserving of its name.
  13 Camden Passage, N1 8EA.
  www.ifeelsmug.com

- **Adventures in Furniture**
  A jewel in Upper Street's interior design crown, AIF specialises in handmade, sustainable furniture built to last a lifetime.
  281 Upper Street, N1 2TZ.
  www.aif.london

- **Sefton**
  APC, Acne Studios and Comme des Garçons sit next to Sefton's own label line in this agenda-setting menswear boutique.
  196 Upper Street, N1 1RQ.
  www.seftonfashion.com

- **Cass Art**
  A mecca for art students and hobbyists, Cass Art's three-floor flagship boasts more colours, crafts and canvasses than you can shake an easel at.
  66-67 Colebrooke Row, N1 8AB.
  www.cassart.co.uk

BOUVERIE ROAD

EDWARD'S LANE

STOKE NEWINGTON CHURCH STREET

STOKE NEWINGTON HIGH STREET

OLIVE LOVES ALFIE

ALBION ROAD

1

2 4

2

3

5

Stoke Newington Church Street

1	THE RESTORATION	4	OLIVE LOVES ALFIE
2	HUB	5	ROUGE
3	STRUT		

STOKE NEWINGTON CHURCH STREET

What happens when the trendy kids who once inhabited
the grittier parts of Hackney grow up, settle down and
want a place to raise their even trendier offspring?
They move to Stoke Newington. Thanks to its detachment
from the tube network, Stokey, as it is affectionately known,
is the preserve of the locals — and crucially, local
businesses. With its quaint village feel and large number of
young families, the area is peppered with chic homeware stores
and cool kids' shops. Most of the action can be found on the
boutique-and-café-lined Church Street — the nicer, better
behaved cousin of the High Street. But thanks to its off-beat
boutiques the latter is well worth a visit too. Stokey may be
tricky to get to but navigate the congested bus journey up
Kingsland Road and you won't regret it.

◀ THE RESTORATION

Don't pass up the opportunity to scour the carefully selected vintage furniture at The Restoration. In a large Victorian stable block across the street from The Cobbled Yard – another must-visit for flatpack-phobes – you will find a treasure trove of reconditioned finds from spotlight theatre lamps to former factory stools.

—

Unit 1 Bouverie Mews, 2 Bouverie Road, N16 0AJ.
07990 573 889
www.the-restoration.com

HUB

Hub has been dressing Stokey's café-hopping residents for almost fifteen years. Threads by Danish label Ganni and France's Sessùn are always in good supply, as is the shop's own knitwear line Allsea. Across the road at number 88 you'll also find a dedicated menswear Hub shop which deals a solid trade in boys clothes by Our Legacy and YMC among others.

—

49 Stoke Newington Church Street, N16 0AR.
020 7254 4494
www.hubshop.co.uk

▲ STRUT

Far from your average thrift shop, Strut's three rooms are bursting with designer garb from the 1930s to the early noughties, tastefully arranged into colour-coded clusters. Owner and veteran vintage buyer Hoana Poland has spent years trawling flea markets for luxury labels, so don't be surprised if your rummage is rewarded with a Chanel or Celia Birtwell original.

—

182 Stoke Newington Church Street, N16 0JL.
020 7254 4387
No website.

OLIVE LOVES ALFIE

Catering to Stoke Newington's stylish pint-sized customers and their picky parents is no mean feat, but it's something which Olive Loves Alfie manages with a flourish. There's a well-chosen mix of kidswear – Mini Rodini, Bobo Choses and Bobux – for ages 0 to 14, together with craft sets, storybooks and playful interior design pieces. A small range of accessories for the grown-ups seals the deal.

—

84 Stoke Newington Church Street, N16 0AP.
020 7241 4212
www.olivelovesalfie.co.uk

ROUGE ▶

For a taste of the Orient that goes beyond China Town's lucky cats, seek out this colourful little shop. Whether you're in the market for an ornate vintage cabinet from Gansu or delicate handpainted ceramics, this shop is packed with authentic pieces that shopkeeper Lei Yang brings back from her native China. Note: Of Cabbages & Kings up the road at number 127 is also a hotspot for unique and thoughtful gifts.

—

158 Stoke Newington High Street, N16 7JL.
020 7275 0887
www.rouge-shop.co.uk

FOUR MORE

- **Nook**
  A small yet serene shop full of beautiful and useful things. Kitchenware is a speciality, while the range of niche magazines invite you to linger for longer.
  153 Stoke Newington Church Street, N16 0UH. www.nookshop.co.uk

- **Only Fools and Peacocks**
  Sisters Claire and Laura Peacock are the brains behind this weird and wonderful fancy dress boutique. Upcycled costumes and eclectic originals are available to rent or buy. Plus the prop-filled basement can be hired out for parties.
  120 Stoke Newington High Street, N16 7NY. www.onlyfoolsandpeacocks.com

- **Prep Cook Shop**
  From terracotta wine coolers to Netherton Foundry frying pans, this independent cook shop offers design-conscious wares that are not for hiding in the kitchen cupboard.
  106 Stoke Newington Church Street, N16 0LA. www.prepcookshop.co.uk

- **Search & Rescue**
  A shop of oddities and curiosities, you're as likely to find a fully-functioning pinball machine here as you are beautifully-designed stationery.
  129 Stoke Newington Church Street, N16 0UH. www.searchandrescuelondon.co.uk

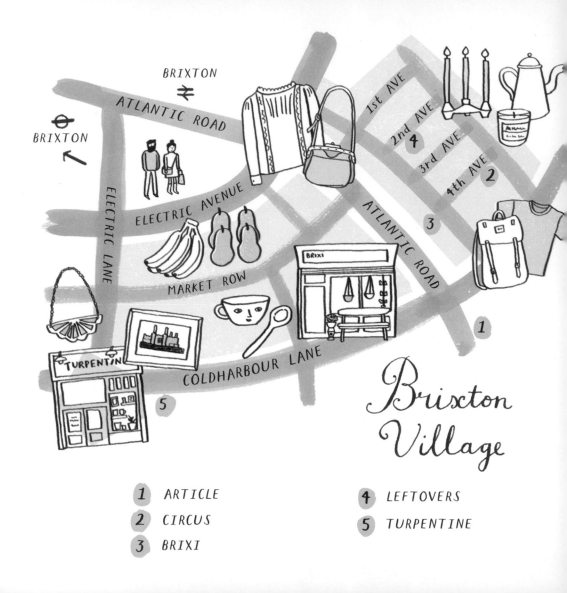

BRIXTON

ATLANTIC ROAD

BRIXTON

1st AVE
2nd AVE
3rd AVE
4th AVE

ELECTRIC LANE

ELECTRIC AVENUE

MARKET ROW

ATLANTIC ROAD

BRIXI

COLDHARBOUR LANE

TURPENTINE

Brixton Village

1 ARTICLE
2 CIRCUS
3 BRIXI
4 LEFTOVERS
5 TURPENTINE

BRIXTON VILLAGE

There are few better places in London to spend your time
and money than Brixton. In fact, this South London hotspot
is so good for shopping it has even got its own currency.
The Brixton Pound, accepted by 250 businesses in the area,
was launched in 2009 and is designed to keep cash circulating
within the community. Two 1930s arcades, Brixton Village and
the adjacent Market Row, are the main shopping hotspots. Both
were saved from demolition thanks to a campaign run by local
residents, and now serve as home to a host of shops in which
old-world curiosities meet modern streetwear. And that's before
you even start on the food...

ARTICLE

The wealth of understated and well-priced streetwear labels is just one of the reasons why this menswear store continues to pull in a steady flow of shoppers. The rest is down to its artfully cool construction. Nested under a railway arch, Article's second branch (the first is on Dalston's Kingsland Road), ticks every box in the hip boutique handbook. The curved, corrugated metal roof and Scandi-minimalist strip lighting gives Brixton's creative industry types a shop to admire, while the cycle-friendly Sandqvist backpacks and cheap Dickies chinos help to ensure they reach the till. The star of the show is Article's hidden shoe room, which features a host of highly Instagrammable features, from the distinctive wood sculpture to the colour-coordinated selection of kicks.

—

61 Atlantic Road, SW9 8PU.
020 7274 5714
www.urbanexcess.com

CIRCUS ▶

A trailblazer in Brixton Village's regeneration, this shoebox-sized cubby is furnished with vintage vases, a library of handmade books and an exceptional assortment of art. It's not uncommon to find a genuine Picasso hanging on the wall here. Plus there's a 'Man Corner' for more macho knick-knacks.

—

Unit 79, Brixton Village, SW9 8PS.
No phone.
www.circusbrixton.com

BRIXI

Not all shops are born out of necessity. Witness Brixi: a shoppable museum of artefacts sourced by self-confessed junk shop addict Emy Gray, which span the ridiculous to the sublime. This mish-mash of knick-knacks never fails to throw up entirely unnecessary but instantly essential trinkets, from unicorn cake toppers to framed dioramas.

—

Unit 40, Brixton Village, SW9 8PR.
07919 162 428
www.brixi.co.uk

LEFTOVERS ▶

One of the 30 original stores chosen to fill a once vacant Brixton Village arcade, Leftovers is distinguished by the rack of antique white blouses, nightgowns and linens displayed outside. Gallic owner Margot Waggoner-Prabhu sources her collection of vintage lace dresses, cotton petticoats, belt buckles, buttons and costume jewels from Paris and the Cote D'Azur.

—

Unit 71, Brixton Village, SW9 8PR.
No phone.
www.leftoverslondon.com

TURPENTINE

Exhibiting the work of more than 80 emerging designers, this artist hub showcases its wealth of prints and ceramics like an art gallery, but without a hint of stuffiness. There are also a host of inclusive in-store workshops, from life drawing to jewellery making.

—

433 Coldharbour Lane, SW9 8LN.
020 3302 7860
www.theturpentine.com

FOUR MORE

- **The Keep Boutique**
  Born out of a frustration with fast fashion, this sustainability-conscious boutique is filled with clothes made to be loved forever.
  Unit 32/33, Brixton Village, SW9 8PR.
  www.thekeepboutique.com

- **Bookmongers**
  Throughout Brixton's changing landscape, Patrick Kelly and his beloved dog Rosa have captained this second-hand bookshop for over two decades.
  439 Coldharbour Lane, SW9 8LN.
  www.bookmongers.com

- **Woo Woo Boutique**
  A word of warning to all tomboys: this sequin-strewn vintage emporium is a purveyor of all things unashamedly girly. Expect tea-dresses and embroidered kimonos aplenty.
  Unit 97, Brixton Village, SW9 8PS.
  www.woowooboutique.co.uk

- **Joy**
  This popular fashion chain started life on neighbouring Coldharbour Lane. Now its store on Brixton Road lives up to its name with daft gifts designed to make you smile.
  518 Brixton Road, SW9 8EN.
  www.joythestore.com

PECKHAM RYE

CHADWICK ROAD

GENERAL STORE 174

GROCERIES   PROVISIONS

COOK

2 CHOUMERT ROAD

BELLENDEN ROAD

1

4   3

5 MAXTED ROAD

Bellenden Road

1 GENERAL STORE   4 THREADS
2 REVIEW   5 MELANGE
3 BIAS

BELLENDEN ROAD

As little as a decade ago, no-one was talking about Peckham. Now, every hot new place to eat, drink, shop and do seems to orbit SE15. Much of its appeal lies in geography, with two opposing streets running parallel and offering a very different perspective of South London life. There's the rough-and-tumble of Rye Lane, with its dance-til-dawn pool halls and late night chicken shops. Then there's the genteel, leafy micro-suburb of Bellenden Road. The latter kick-started the area's increasing influence and affluence with just three businesses: the Petitou café, the former fashion emporium Fenton Walsh and the still-going-strong Review bookshop. Now it's got a fair few more for city adventurers to visit.

GENERAL STORE

A cut far above your average corner shop, this delicatessen caters to the area's quinoa-and-kale-munching classes with its supply of fresh, seasonal produce and fancy store cupboard essentials or foodie gifts. Locally and London-sourced fodder includes sourdough loaves from Brixton's BreadBread Bakery and artisanal Mexican cheese from Old Kent Road's Gringa Dairy.

—

174 Bellenden Road, SE15 4BW.
020 7642 2129
www.generalsto.re

REVIEW

Opened by two Peckham locals in 2005 and now run by prize-winning novelist Evie Wyld, this friendly, independent bookshop prides itself on cherry-picking every title in the shop, which has a strong skew towards contemporary fiction and a section reserved for signed first editions. It also hosts the annual Peckham Literary Festival.

—

131 Bellenden Road, SE15 4QY.

0207 639 7400

www.reviewbookshop.co.uk

BIAS ▶

Leaving behind a thirty-year teaching career, owner Sally took a leap of faith and opened Bias in 2012. The result is a shop which includes the sorts of luxury labels you'd expect to find in a high-end Chelsea haunt (Baum und Pferdgarten, Bellerose, MiH), coupled with a dedication to local designers and Peckham-produced ethical homeware.

—

143 Bellenden Rd, SE15 4DH.
020 7732 3747
www.biasboutique.com

THREADS

Since taking over this well-established vintage fashion boutique in 2014, Savile Row-trained eco-fashion designer Jemima Norton has been busy supplementing its second-hand stock with new pieces from independent local designers. Look out for the bright geometric jackets by Koro Kimono and the store's own line of made-in-Peckham accessories and repro retro clobber.

—

186 Bellenden Road, SE15 4BW.
020 3784 0020
www.threadspeckham.com

MELANGE

Ask anyone in South London where to get a sugar fix and the answer is always the same: Melange. As if straight out of the pages of Joanne Harris's *Chocolat*, Parisienne owner and self-taught chocolatier Isabelle Alaya set up shop in 2008 and has been giving Peckham's chocolate-lovers a place to indulge their sweet tooth ever since. As well as offering a host of workshops – from chocolate painting to wine pairing – Melange specialises in hand layered slabs of dark, milk and white chocolate with unique flavour combinations such as ginger and lime and raspberry and rosemary. Stop short of gorging yourself on the sample trays to save room for the café's signature hot chocolates, voted the best in London by the capital's most meticulous chocoholics. Try the delicious coconut milk option, whether you're vegan or not.

—

2 Maxted Road, SE15 4LL.
07722 650 711
www.themelange.com

FOUR MORE

- **Quaint & Belle**
  Liverpudlian former fashion illustrator Jacqueline pedals a lovely brand of flotsam and jetsam for the home, from glassware and gifts to cards and candles.
  144 Bellenden Road, SE15 4RF.
  No website.

- **Worn Not Torn**
  This second-hand thrift shop houses a seemingly never-ending supply of old cases, chests and trunks. Get elbow-deep in the jumble to uncover the best hidden gems.
  149 Bellenden Road, SE15 4DH.
  No website.

- **Flock & Herd**
  As with all good gentrified London thoroughfares, Bellenden Road is home to an artisan butcher. Offering rare breed meats and choice cuts, Flock & Herd is the perfect place to pick up a roasting joint to impress your friends.
  155 Bellenden Road, SE15 4DH.
  www.flockandherd.com

- **Persepolis**
  Sally Butcher – owner and author of four cookbooks including *Snackistan* and *Persia in Peckham* – brings Middle Eastern fare to the heart of South London in this brilliantly bonkers café-cum-deli.
  28-30 Peckham High Street, SE15 5DT.
  www.foratasteofpersia.co.uk

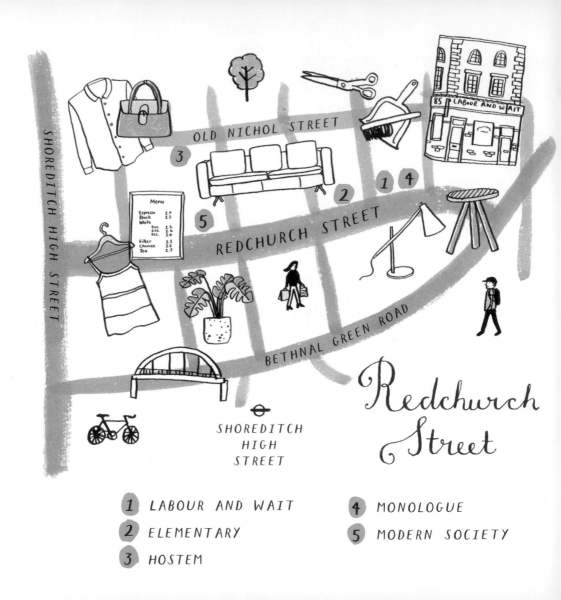

SHOREDITCH HIGH STREET

OLD NICHOL STREET

85 LABOUR AND WAIT

REDCHURCH STREET

Menu

Espresso 2.0
Black 2.5
White
4oz. 2.2
6oz. 2.4
8oz. 3.0

Filter 2.5
Chemex 3.5
Tea 2.5

BETHNAL GREEN ROAD

SHOREDITCH
HIGH
STREET

Redchurch
Street

1 LABOUR AND WAIT
2 ELEMENTARY
3 HOSTEM
4 MONOLOGUE
5 MODERN SOCIETY

REDCHURCH STREET

There are many preconceptions surrounding this street, the highest rung of hipster-cool in Shoreditch: there's the dogs more groomed than show day at Crufts; the freelance graphic designers with Macbook Airs tucked under their tattooed arms; and the denim-clad coffee breakers enquiring as to the provenance of their £5 pour over. And then there's beards.

So many beards. And while Redchurch Street lives up to expectation, hipster haters should write this *Vogue*-endorsed shopping street off at their peril. As London's premier design district, it's a magnet for cult labels that have enough of a following to fend off rising rents, as well as big brands with the clout required to cash in on its cool. Just ask Donatella Versace, who opened an outpost for her diffusion Versus label here. It's also home to the emerging London trend for coffee bars in shops, meaning that for keen beans intent on stopping by, a serious shopping buzz is guaranteed.

LABOUR AND WAIT

The Labour and Wait story sprung from an unlikely source: a dustpan and brush. Disillusioned by their jobs as menswear designers, founders Rachel Wythe-Moran and Simon Watkins decided instead to turn their creative nous into perfecting everyday household objects for the twenty-first century home. Their simple and stylish approach to practicality has turned shopping for doorstops and dishcloths into a wholly pleasurable pursuit. Behind the shop's green brick façade (the former home of Truman Brewery pub The Dolphin), lies a cornucopia of ostrich-feather dusters, non-drip French candles and beautifully-packaged screwdriver sets, the likes of which no self-respecting Shoreditch homestead would be without.

—

85 Redchurch Street, E2 7DJ.
020 7729 6253
www.labourandwait.co.uk

ELEMENTARY ▶

More like an art gallery than a shop, Elementary deals in aesthetically-pleasing objects for showroom-worthy homes. Designs from Japan and Scandinavia with a distinctly clutter-repellent air are displayed next to the store's own handcrafted Editions range. Expect impeccable taste, eye-watering prices and a sudden urge to throw out all of your possessions and start again.

—

77 Redchurch Street, E2 7DJ.

020 3487 0980

www.elementarystore.co.uk

HOSTEM

Part uber-luxury menswear boutique, part feat of architectural brilliance, Hostem's behemoth five-storey HQ has become a cult retail destination for the world's most discerning shoppers. Head downstairs to the low-lit basement for one-of-a-kind investment pieces, or venture up to the lofty, light-filled galleries to take your pick from next season's Comme des Garçons and Loewe.

—

28 Old Nichol Street, E2 7HR.

020 7739 9733

www.hostem.co.uk

MONOLOGUE ▶

Despite occupying just 50 square feet of Redchurch Street, it's easy to get lost in interior designer Pavel Klimczak's dinky concept store. Brimming with stylish accessories with a Scandi slant – think HAY stationery and strokeably soft throws by Mae Engelgeer – each item invites close inspection, resulting in a high-end design store which is as accessible as it is aspirational.

—

93 Redchurch Street, E2 7DJ.

020 7729 0400

www.monologuelondon.com

MODERN SOCIETY

This luxury general store is home to two of East London's most prized possessions: good clothes and great coffee. Browse the ever-expanding roll-call of emerging designers (particularly the embroidered leather jackets by Sandy Liang), or pull up a pew at the tiny four-stool café bar, which gives shoppers a place to perch and admire the brilliant edit of photography prints on the walls.

—

33 Redchurch Street, E2 7DJ.
020 7729 0311
www.themodernsociety.com

FOUR MORE

- **Klaus Haapaniemi**
  The first and only showroom for acclaimed
  Finnish textiles designers Klaus Haapaniemi
  and Mia Wallenius. Head here for silk brocade
  cushions and premium tufted wool rugs.
  81 Redchurch Street, E2 7DJ.
  www.klaush.com

- **Sunspel**
  This 150-year-old heritage British clothing
  manufacturer was the first firm to introduce
  boxer shorts to the UK. Now their soft navy
  sweatshirts and cotton crew neck tees are a
  staple in the uniform of East London's menfolk.
  7 Redchurch Street, E2 7DJ.
  www.sunspel.com

- **Mast Brothers**
  An artisanal chocolate shop hailing from Brooklyn,
  Mast Brothers smells as good as it
  looks and offers exquisitely-packaged bars
  and daily micro-factory tours.
  19-29 Redchurch Street, E2 7DJ.
  www.mastbrothers.com

- **By Walski**
  A unique shop specialising in action sports
  camera equipment. The store also houses
  surfwear and hosts regular extreme sports video
  screenings for city-dwelling adrenaline junkies.
  59 Redchurch Street, E2 7DJ.
  www.by-walski.com

CLAPTON

POWERSCROFT ROAD

CHATSWORTH ROAD

LOWER CLAPTON ROAD

CLIFDEN ROAD

HOMERTON

Lower Clapton Road
&
Chatsworth Road

1 BOTANY

2 TRIANGLE

3 BRAHMS & LISZT

4 LION COFFEE + RECORDS

5 BAD DENIM

LOWER CLAPTON ROAD
& CHATSWORTH ROAD

As far as radical transformations go, few places can compete
with Clapton. Chatsworth Road, together with the parallel Lower
Clapton Road, was once considered among the most dangerous
areas of London. Now it's a haven of galleries, cafés and
brilliant boutiques frequented by the edgiest of East London
dwellers, as well as young families who got in before the prices
sky rocketed. As one of the capital's longest high streets,
Chatsworth Road is marked out by its large concentration of
independent shops, many of which are run by passionate locals.
Among the finest feathers in its cap are tequila den Brahms &
Liszt, the great jeans at Bad Denim and a Sunday food market
which is good enough to compete with the popular
Broadway Market as Hackney's finest.

BOTANY

This charming plant and homeware store brings together city-friendly foliage and fair trade ceramics. With an ethical and community-minded emphasis, the shop also offers wildflower arranging workshops and stocks supplies from local makers including Pip Hartle pottery and bags by Bramble & Mr Twigg.

—

5 Chatsworth Road, E5 0LH
020 3759 8191
www.botanyshop.co.uk

TRIANGLE

Conceived by three friends – Tori, Mary and Matthew – with a shared love of good design, Triangle stocks all the barometers of taste (HAY stationery, Fig + Yarrow bath soaks, Form & Thread striped tees) alongside a constant flow of quality mid-century vintage furniture, all of which makes for the sort of shop you could snap up in its entirety.

---

81 Chatsworth Road, E5 0LH.
020 8510 9361
www.trianglestore.co.uk

BRAHMS & LISZT

Vying for attention amongst Hackney's many independent bottle shops is no easy task, but Brahms & Liszt has a particularly distinctive USP: tequila. And lots of it. Owner Melanie Symonds – the brains behind small batch brand Quiquiriqui Mezcal – and her liquor-loving team know everything there is to know about Mexican spirit and this off-licence with a difference flogs rare mezcal and tequila in decadent prohibition-style surroundings. But there's much on offer for any discerning drinker. The shop also boasts wine-on-tap and ready-made cocktail stations alongside a wide range of ingredients and equipment for budding mixologists. For a crash course in all things intoxicating, sign up for one of their legendary tasting sessions and you'll soon discover why it shares its name with the cockney rhyming slang for drunk.

—

10 Chatsworth Road, E5 0LP.
07946 461 616
www.brahmsandlisztlondon.uk

LION COFFEE + RECORDS ▶

Cool vinyl and hot coffee combine in this café-
cum-venue-cum-record-shop. Set up by a group
of music aficionados, including Florence & the
Machine drummer Christopher Lloyd Hayden and
record label owner Mairead Nash, Lion Coffee +
Records is as good for spinning records as it is for
spotting newly signed acts.

—

118 Lower Clapton Road, E5 0QR.
020 8986 7372
www.lioncoffeerecords.com

BAD DENIM

Don't be fooled by the name, this specialist denim
den sells anything but. Owner Erin McQuinn –
who honed her knowledge of great jeans at brands
including MiH Jeans and Victoria Beckham –
arranges her edit by style rather than brand and
stocks high-end labels alongside rare vintage finds
that she sources herself.

—

82 Lower Clapton Road, E5 0RN.
020 7993 9019
www.baddenim.co.uk

FOUR MORE

- **The Hackney Draper**
  This haberdashery for the twenty-first century
  is cult amongst those seeking to decorate with a
  difference. The Hackney Draper is as scrupulous
  about soft furnishings as it is colour schemes
  courtesy of its own paint line.
  25 Chatsworth Road, E5 0LH.
  www.thehackneydraper.co.uk

- **Everything But The Dog**
  Specialists in restored mid-century furniture and
  service with a smile, Everything But The Dog was
  so named because everything in the store is for
  sale apart from the beloved shop dog Billy.
  65 Chatsworth Road, E5 0LH.
  www.everythingbutthedog.eu

- **Pages of Hackney**
  The real beauty of this independent bookshop
  lies in the basement, which is home to squidgy
  sofas and an unrivalled collection of second-hand
  Penguin classics.
  70 Lower Clapton Road, E5 0RN.
  www.pagesofhackney.co.uk

- **London Borough of Jam**
  Former St John pastry chef turned jam maker
  Lillie O'Brien has converted her passion for
  preserves into an oasis of sticky sweet delicacies
  and local craft beer. Open only at weekends.
  51D Chatsworth Road, E5 0LH.
  www.londonboroughofjam.com

HOXTON

SHIPTON STREET

RAVENSCROFT ROAD

COLUMBIA ROAD

EZRA ROAD

96 ANGELA FLANDERS 96

SHOREDITCH HIGH STREET

Columbia Road

1 ANGELA FLANDERS
2 CHOOSING KEEPING
3 B SOUTHGATE
4 NOM LIVING
5 DANDY STAR

COLUMBIA ROAD

For a snapshot of East London during Queen Victoria's reign,
take a walk down Columbia Road. With its cobbled side streets
and chocolate box shop fronts, it is the ultimate stroll down
memory lane. In its previous life the street was a pathway
along which sheep were driven to the abattoir at Smithfield.
Nowadays, Columbia Road is best known for its famous Sunday
flower market that transforms the thoroughfare into a tangle of
tulips and tourists. During the rest of the week things are just
as picturesque. Behind the antiquated exteriors are a diverse
selection of retailers — some traditional, others markedly
modern — which makes this pocket of Hackney an essential stop
for visitors and locals alike.

ANGELA FLANDERS

The late, great Angela Flanders opened her first artisan perfume shop on Columbia Road in 1985, and her legacy lives on in the beautiful boutique now run by her daughter Kate Evans, who also owns chic Shoreditch fashion boutique Precious. The lovingly restored and delightfully chintzy nineteenth-century shop stocks the full range of 40 scents that the self-taught perfumer created during her lifetime. Captivating, woody fragrances are an Angela Flanders signature, such as the spicy Bois de Seville or her newest scent Columbia Rose, created in homage to the old East End. Angela also opened a second store in Spitalfields' Artillery Passage in 2012. Open only at weekends.

—

96 Columbia Road, E2 7QB.
020 7739 7555
www.angelaflanders-perfumer.com

CHOOSING KEEPING

This quaint little shop is catnip for stationery fetishists, gift-hunters and digital-refuseniks. Proprietress Julia, who spent her early years in France and Tokyo, has a keen eye for all things miniature, from the practical (leather-bound notebooks, wooden pencil trays) to the pretty (ceramic bird paperweights, hand-blown hourglasses). It's near impossible to leave without a new desk mate.

—

128 Columbia Road, E2 7RG.
020 7613 3842
www.choosingkeeping.com

◄ B SOUTHGATE

Furniture restorer Ben Southgate has amassed a loyal following among East London's design elite. Open 9am–4pm on Sundays only, this stylish man cave is filled with sumptuous leather armchairs and handsome oak chests, which he tends to from his workshop barn in East Sussex. Vintage board games and German anatomical models are also worthy points of interest.

—

4 The Courtyard, Ezra Street, E2 7RH.
07905 960 792
www.bsouthgate.co.uk

NOM LIVING

Working directly with artisans in Vietnam and Cambodia, Nom Living offers beautifully rustic kitchenware for eco-conscious homes. Bamboo placemats, coconut wood spoons and hand thrown clay bowls are among its signature sustainable essentials. Its cinnamon bark boxes not only offer a stylish storage solution for sugar and coffee, they also infuse their contents with a spicy aroma.

—

102 Columbia Road, E2 7QB.
07976 917 265
www.nomliving.com

DANDY STAR

Thanks to Dandy Star's rainbow-painted front, the latest addition to Columbia Road is also one of the brightest. Venture inside this kids' boutique and things are just as vibrant. Its trademark graphic tees are cult among London's style-conscious parents and their achingly cool offspring, while its growing homeware offering decorates the bedrooms of kids who prefer Bowie to Bieber.

—

126 Columbia Road, E2 7RG.
020 7613 1510
www.dandystar.com

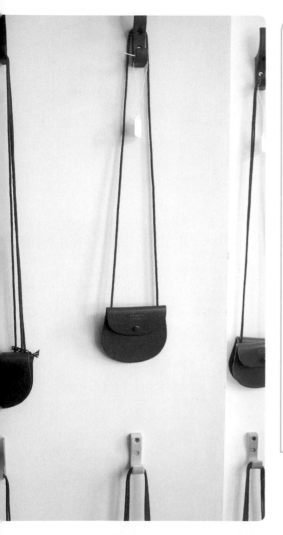

FOUR MORE

- **Bob & Blossom**
  From knitted animals and wooden spinning tops to striped romper suits, nostalgia wins out in this charming children's shop. Open only at weekends.
  140 Columbia Road, E2 7RG.
  www.bobandblossom.co.uk

- **Two Columbia Road**
  This spacious gallery specialises in collectable furniture (Hans Wegner, Finn Juhl) and contemporary art (Patrick Caulfield, Marc Quinn). Gilbert and George are among its fans.
  2 Columbia Road, E2 7NN.
  www.twocolumbiaroad.co.uk

- **Harry Brand**
  A quirky weekend gift shop selling its own-brand Harissa chilli sauce alongside woollen picnic blankets and solar-powered Waving Queens.
  122 Columbia Road, E2 7RG.
  www.harrybrand.co.uk

- **Nelly Duff**
  A gallery and exhibition space showcasing prints from the worlds of graphic, tattoo and street art. Works by Eine and Banksy are regulars here.
  156 Columbia Road, E2 7RG.
  www.nellyduff.com

Golborne Road

1 FOUND AND VISION

2 FEZ

3 PHOENIX ON GOLBORNE

4 RELLIK

5 GOLDFINGER FACTORY

WORNINGTON ROAD

GOLBORNE ROAD

PORTOBELLO ROAD

ELKSTONE ROAD

WESTBOURNE PARK

LADBROKE GROVE

GOLBORNE ROAD

Of the capital's many skills is its ability to condense
entire cities, countries and cultures into a few streets.
The south-western corner of Clerkenwell is home to Little
Italy. Little Venice can be found just north of Paddington.
And underneath Notting Hill's iconic Trellik Tower you'll find
Little Morocco, so named for its wealth of Moroccan restaurants,
shops selling Maghrebian wares and its surprising ability to
resist gentrification – despite its close proximity to the
tourist trap of Portobello Road. Golborne Road wears a badge
of honest authenticity, which is hard to match anywhere else
in the capital. Its retail premises are endearingly ramshackle
and devoted to fabric shops, vintage fashion outposts, antiques
emporiums and community-driven enterprises, many of
which have been trading here for years.

FOUND AND VISION

A choice haunt among London's most famous vintage fanatics – from Kate Moss to Sienna Miller and Florence Welch – Found and Vision is a jewel in the crown of Notting Hill's second-hand shopping scene. Founded by stylist Karen Clarkson, who opened the boutique with friends Oxana Korsun and Rosie Meres in 2013, this bricks and mortar dressing up box has become the go-to hunting ground for rare designer threads from Yves Saint Laurent couture to Seventies Missoni classics. But with shoppers including savvy stylists scouring for their next magazine shoot, the stock rarely stays put for long.

---

104 Golborne Road, W10 5PS.
020 3620 5755
www.foundandvision.com

◄ FEZ

This Aladdin's cave of well-priced Moroccan imports is like stepping into the heart of a medina without crossing the M25. Owner Omar Serroukh, who has called the capital home since 1986, travels back to his native country three times a year to stockpile leather slippers, hand-woven carpets, tagines and decorative lanterns to furnish his jam-packed bazaar.

—

71 Golborne Road, W10 5NP.
020 8964 5573
No website.

PHOENIX ON GOLBORNE

Eschewing the dusty, cramped antique store set-up in favour of a light, bright and inviting space, Jess Gildersleve's vintage furniture finds are displayed in full glory. Decorative mirrors are something of a speciality here, as are shabby-chic French dressers, velvet chaise lounges and spectacular chandeliers. Downstairs is home to a collection of cherry-picked vintage womenswear.

—

67 Golborne Road, W10 5NP.
020 8964 8123
www.phoenixongolborne.co.uk

▲ RELLIK

A favourite among fashion industry insiders, Rellik is hailed as one of the capital's best high-end vintage shops. It's ideal if you're looking for something really special from the 1920s or 1930s, and equally good for classic 1950s clobber. The likes of Kylie Minogue and Lady Gaga have been through the doors to browse its stash of golden era Chloe and Ossie Clark.

—

8 Golborne Road, W10 5NW.
020 8962 0089
www.relliklondon.co.uk

GOLDFINGER FACTORY

Named after Erno Goldfinger – the architect who designed the iconic Trellik Tower in which it resides – Goldfinger Factory brings the Midas touch to cast-off furniture by training local artisans-in-the-making in the art of upcycling. Along with a showroom and café, its social enterprise programme also encompasses workshops on carpentry, paint effects and DIY.

—

13-15 Golborne Road, W10 5NY.
020 3302 0900
www.goldfingerfactory.com

FOUR MORE

- **Honest Jon's**
  Established in 1974, Johnny Rotten and Malcolm McLaren were once regulars at this venerable record shop which specialises in bebop, reggae, jazz and funk.
  278 Portobello Road, W10 5TE.
  www.honestjons.com

- **Jane Bourvis**
  A vintage bridal boudoir bursting at the seams with antique lace gowns, boned silk corsets and strings of pearls. Twenties and 1930s styles influence much of the dresses on offer. By appointment only.
  89 Golborne Road, W10 5NL.
  www.janebourvis.co.uk

- **88 Antiques**
  A veteran on Golborne Road's antiques scene, Dave Lucas has been peddling reclaimed wood furniture at number 88 for over 30 years.
  88 Golborne Road, W10 5PS.
  www.88antiques.com

- **Ally Cappellino West**
  A quality British accessories label whose timeless panniers and rucksacks give the latest It bag a run for its money. The brand also has stores in Shoreditch and Marylebone.
  312 Portobello Road, W10 5RU.
  www.allycapellino.co.uk

LADBROKE GROVE

WESTBOURNE PARK ROAD

BOOKS for COOKS

KENSINGTON PARK ROAD

COLVILLE TERRACE

LEDBURY ROAD

WESTBOURNE GROVE

NOTTING HILL GATE

Westbourne Grove

1 COUVERTURE & GARBSTONE

2 BOOKS FOR COOKS

3 CARAMEL

4 AIMÉ

5 NATIVE & CO

WESTBOURNE GROVE

Those wishing to locate the polar opposite of Golborne
Road's rough and tumble, or the tourist-swamped Portobello
Road, don't have to journey very far. Notting Hill's other
shopping enclave — Westbourne Grove and its surrounding
streets — offer a bounty of fashion boutiques packed out with
high-end labels and even higher price tags, as well as a cluster
of cafés teeming with monied, blow-dried types. Much like its
shoppers, Westbourne Grove and Ledbury Road love labels, while
nearby Kensington Park Road is a must-see for those with the
hots for homeware. Come here if you want to have your pick
of West London finery — and bring your AMEX.

COUVERTURE & THE GARBSTORE

Housed in a converted period townhouse, this cult concept store makes you feel like you're wandering around an (exceptionally tasteful) living room. Set across three floors, this Notting Hill haven is actually two shops sandwiched together. The ground and galleried first floors make up Couverture and are dedicated to womenswear from strictly independent labels plus jewellery, accessories, kidswear and the odd piece of furniture. Meanwhile the basement is home to menswear brand Garbstore. Here, its own vintage-inspired buys for boys are showcased alongside a good selection of cult international brands, many of which are exclusive to the UK. Both brands are also renowned for sought-after collaborations, which include recent collections with Reebok and American varsity jacket producers Golden Bear.

—

188 Kensington Park Road, W11 2ES.
020 7229 2178
www.couvertureandthegarbstore.com

BOOKS FOR COOKS

Notting Hill stalwart Books For Cooks has become a global destination for foodies. Since 1983, its shelves have been stuffed with cookbooks of every conceivable cuisine and its staff has consisted of former chefs and culinary experts – the most famous of whom was future 'Fat Lady' Clarissa Dickson Wright. It has also earned a reputation as 'the best smelling shop in the world', owing to the tiny kitchen sandwiched between the bookshelves at the back of store where recipes are tested daily and served to hungry shoppers at lunch. Cookery classes are also held in the demonstration kitchen above the shop.

—

4 Blenheim Crescent, W11 1NN.
020 7221 1992
www.booksforcooks.com

◄ CARAMEL

Founder Eva Karayiannis launched Caramel with the aim to provide stylish, well-made childrenswear and a point of difference to mass-produced brands and impractical designer labels. Her designs are now a staple of every Primrose Hill school gate and the brand has recently branched out with a range for mum-sized fans too.

—

77 Ledbury Road, W11 2AG.
020 7727 0906
www.caramel-shop.co.uk

AIMÉ

This renowned boutique is beloved by the capital's Francophiles. Bringing together the most coveted Parisian labels under one roof, Aimé is the best place to source next season's Isabel Marant without having to cross the Channel. Next door you'll also find Petit Aimé — a chic children's offshoot stocked with Bonton babygrows and Vilac wooden toys.

—

32 Ledbury Road, W11 2AB.
020 7221 7070
www.aimelondon.com

NATIVE & CO

Simplicity, craftsmanship and honest materials are at the heart of this popular kitchenware store. Founded by Central Saint Martin's graduates Sharon Jo-Yun Hung and Chris Yoshiro Green, the focus is on design-led products sourced from Japan and Taiwan. The store's cool, calm and collected interior is mirrored by the stock it sells, from traditional fish knives to copper kettles and delicately painted rice bowls.

—

116 Kensington Park Road, W11 2PW.
020 7243 0418
www.nativeandco.com

FOUR MORE

- **Merchant Archive**
  An upscale, fashionable boutique that combines founder Sophie Merchant's passion for high-end vintage pieces with her own contemporary luxury womenswear label.
  19 Kensington Park Road, W11 2EU.
  www.merchantarchive.com

- **Daylesford Notting Hill**
  This organic deli/grocery/bakery/café provides West Londoners with produce direct from its Gloucestershire farm. Try their cold-pressed juices if you're feeling virtuous, or the salted caramel hearts if you're not.
  208-212 Westbourne Grove, W11 2RH.
  www.daylesford.com

- **R.S. Currie & Co**
  It is near impossible to walk past this eccentric toyshop and not venture in. The humbug-striped shop front conceals a cornucopia of play things to delight all under 10 (and many over).
  105 Westbourne Grove, W2 4UW.
  www.rscurrie.com

- **Fara Kids and Baby**
  Arguably the best of Fara charity's thirteen kidswear outlets, namely because it is stocked with premium cast-offs from the area's well-clad sprogs. Expect to find Petit Bateau mariniere tops without so much as a ketchup stain.
  39 Ledbury Road, W11 2AA.
  www.faracharity.org

WOLF & BADGER

This striking boutique provides a platform for an eclectic array of up-and-coming designers such as Bora Aksu, Gyunel and Lucy Choi. A good chunk of space is devoted to its extensive menswear offering, while its basement gallery is reserved for installations and pop ups. The brand's sister store on Ledbury Street is also home to tiny, specialist labels such as pyjama brand Desmond & Dempsey and jewellers Astrid & Miyu.

—

32 Dover Street, W1S 4NE.
020 3627 3191
www.wolfandbadger.com

PAM PAM

Frustrated by the lack of stylish and practical options for women in the male-dominated trainer world, friends Bethany Heggarty and Rio Holland endeavoured to open the UK's first female-only sneaker shop. Nestled between the kebab shops on Bethnal Green Road, Pam Pam offers a tightly edited selection of covetable kicks – from Nike to New Balance – as well as niche labels including Garment Project and Novesta for the passionate sneakerhead.

---

129 Bethnal Green Road, E2 6DG.

020 3601 7860

www.pampamlondon.com

CÉLINE

Under the direction of the industry's favourite minimalist Phoebe Philo, Céline has become the label regularly name-checked by fashion insiders as the one they want to wear. True to its stealth luxury aesthetic, no aspect of its flagship is unconsidered, even down to the marble-and-semi-precious-stone parquet flooring. If you have impeccable taste and several thousand pounds burning a hole in your pocket, truly, there is no better place to spend it.

---

103 Mount Street, W1K 2AP.

020 7491 8200

www.celine.com

VICTORIA BECKHAM

When Victoria Beckham launched her career as a designer in 2008, there were many who scoffed at the former Spice Girl's ambition to make it in the cut-throat world of high fashion. But Posh has succeeded in silencing her critics with her modern, understated breed of luxury womenswear. The VB retail empire on fashionable Dover Street, masterminded by conceptual architect Farshid Moussavi (who also worked on the Olympic Park), was under construction for a year before it opened in 2014 to much fuss and fanfare. The cool concrete construction spans three floors: the entrance is given over to a wall of accessories and her more affordable diffusion line, the top floor is devoted to her catwalk collection and the basement is a personal shopping suite. The proprietress regularly pops in, so shoppers can often get a glimpse of more than just her new season handbags.

—

36 Dover Street, W1S 4NH.
020 7042 0700
www.victoriabeckham.com

CHRISTOPHER KANE ▶

Scottish designer Christopher Kane is the hottest ticket at London Fashion Week and revered for his innovative and rebellious approach to femininity. His Mount Street flagship is a chic embodiment of his fashion-forward aesthetic: clean and minimal with stack shelving displaying structured handbags and glass cabinets to display his museum-worthy creations.

—

6 Mount Street, W1K 3EH.
020 7493 3111
www.christopherkane.com

MATCHESFASHION.COM

Husband and wife team Tom and Ruth Chapman opened their first independent multi-brand boutique – known then as Matches – in 1987 in Wimbledon Village with the aim of being the first to introduce international labels such as Prada and Bottega Veneta to the UK. Now the couple run five boutiques across London and recently rebranded with the '.com' to reflect a global online presence.

—

36 High Street, SW19 5BY.
020 8947 9777
www.matchesfashion.com

AIDA ▶

This Shoreditch boutique is brilliant for discovering chic and affordable indie labels, from the local (Pyrus, Elia B.) to the far-flung (Minimum, Des Petit Hauts). Get your hair done at its vintage beauty parlour, join them for a film screening or grab a coffee in the cute café. Chaps are treated to a wealth of city-friendly separates and made-to-measure suit services by resident tailors J&J Minnis.

—

133 Shoreditch High Street, E1 6JE.
020 7739 2811
www.aidashoreditch.co.uk

DIVERSE

Following three decades on Islington's Upper Street, Saskia Lamche decided to up sticks and relocate her mother's iconic clothing shop to Tufnell Park's increasingly influential Fortess Road. Now, the family-owned boutique continues to give tastemakers their fix of next season APC and Studio Nicholson in friendly, unintimidating surroundings.

—

148 Fortess Road, NW5 2HP.
020 7813 7425
www.diverseclothing.com

& OTHER STORIES

A Swedish high street shopping revolution from the brains behind H&M and COS, & Other Stories offers fashion for those with champagne tastes and beer budgets. Inspired by personal style rather than trends or fast fashion fixes, the chain has more high-fashion credentials than most with design ateliers in Stockholm and Paris. Head there for party dresses, lovely lingerie and statement accessories.

—

256-258 Regent Street, W1B 3AF.
020 3402 9190
www.stories.com

EGG SHOP

This tiny yet enormously influential boutique, run by its famously fastidious founder Maureen Doherty, is one of the capital's most highly rated cult shops among those in the know. Housed in a former dairy, Egg still retains its original blue and white tiles, wooden barn doors and sense of honest authenticity. Its USP is simple and sophisticated clothing with an arty schew, which is designed to be worn and loved forever – a sentiment that is reflected in the steep price tags. Comfort, quality and timelessness are key, with brands such as Sophie D'Hoore, Scha and Casey Casey represented. While nowadays Egg also has an ecommerce site, this is a shop you have to visit in person to appreciate fully. Frequent trips are recommended as Doherty routinely curates her wares as if it were a gallery.

36 Kinnerton Street, SW1X 8ES.
020 7235 9315
www.eggtrading.com

SEE ALSO...
Mouki Mou (p29), Prism (p33), Hub (p45), Bad Denim (p82), Aimé (p109), Merchant Archive (p111)

LET'S HEAR IT FOR THE BOYS MENSWEAR

◄ PRESENT

If you're the sort of bloke who doesn't like to follow the crowd, you will find an affinity with Present. Stocked with a variety of esoteric labels, such as Japan's Haversack and New York shirting brand Rough & Tumble, owners Eddie Prendergast and Steve Davies have an eye for a future classic. Which comes as no surprise – the duo founded ubiquitous 1990s superbrand Duffer of St George.

—

140 Shoreditch High Street, E1 6JE.
020 7033 0500
www.present-london.com

BEGGARS RUN

Having outgrown its original showroom above Bethnal Green's Approach Tavern pub, modern tailoring outfitter Beggars Run have relocated to roomier premises befitting their growing reputation in nearby Old Street. While you won't be able to pick up a pint with your made-to-measure suit, its moleskin bombers and relaxed take on formalwear will keep its customers happy.

—

33A Charlotte Road, EC2A 3PB.
020 8133 3466
www.beggarsrun.com

STUMPER & FIELDING

A beacon of Britishness on one of London's most famous tourist trails, Stumper & Fielding should be a place to avoid. Except it isn't. Instead, this independent modern English outfitters maintains an authenticity and charm which keeps residents coming back time and time again. Head there for Loake shoes, Gloverall duffle coats and the brand's own line of conversation-starting socks.

—

107 Portobello Road, W11 2QB.
020 7229 5577
No website.

DRAKES

A mere cufflink's throw from Savile Row and its suiting stalwarts stands Drakes, a purveyor of final flourishes prized by the Mayfair gentry for its handmade ties and silk pocket squares. Close attention to detail is continued in the shop fit, with Harris Tweed armchairs and cabinets procured from the Natural History Museum. A second shop is located under its factory in Hoxton.

—

3 Clifford Street, W1S 2LF.
020 7734 2367
www.drakes.com

◄ PERCIVAL

Renowned for its understated aesthetic and dedication to British manufacturing, this popular label made Soho's pre-eminent menswear hive Berwick Street its home in 2012. After you've scoured the rails of tailored coach jackets, custom-print shirts and no-nonsense knitwear, don't miss cult trainer hub Foot Patrol at number 80 and Nudie Jeans Repair Shop around the corner on D'Arblay Street.

—

43 Berwick Street, W1F 8SB.
020 7734 4533
www.percivalclo.com

ALBAM

James Shaw and Alastair Rae opened their first store on Beak Street under the guise of a six-month pop up. Fast-forward seven years and Albam's brand of honest design and high-end basics has earned legions of fans and three more outposts in the capital. Among its most popular purchases are its flight bags, selvedge denim jeans and the holy grail of any man's wardrobe – the perfect t-shirt.

—

23 Beak Street, W1F 9RS.
020 3157 7000
www.albamclothing.com

PALACE

The kids who spent their youth grinding rails and wearing DCs have grown up, got proper jobs and upgraded their taste to Palace. The homegrown hyper-cool skate empire has secured cult status in the streetwear world with its ultra-limited edition hoodies. At its Soho store – think monochrome marble floors and minimal rails of clothing – expect to queue alongside superfans for the latest t-shirt drop.

—

26 Brewer Street, W1F 0SW.
020 7287 5048
www.palaceskateboards.com

MR START

Following a brief hiatus in 2015, retail veteran Philip Start has reopened the doors of his iconic Hoxton emporium. First appearing on Rivington Street in 2008, this modern British sartorialist has long been East London's answer to Savile Row. Its just-the-right-side-of-slim-fit suits are complemented by a range of knitted ties and factory shirts, which are crucial to cracking the elusive smart/casual dress code.

—

40 Rivington Street, EC2A 3LX.
020 7729 6272
www.mr-start.com

O'DELL'S

The popularity of this modern man's boutique
has seen it graduate from Shoreditch-secret to
Soho-staple. But rest assured its local-minded
mentality remains intact; from simple pleasures
– cold-pressed coffee, organic beard oil – to
more extravagant purchases like a made-to-order
rucksack or a handwoven rug by Pimlico resident
Rachel Scott, an obsessive attention to detail
ensures a high standard across the board.

—

7 Green's Court, W1F 0HQ.
07730 129 416
www.odellsstore.com

OI POLLOI

Bringing a dash of Northern Soul to the heart of London, seminal Manchester menswear boutique Oi Polloi opened its first store outside its hometown in 2015. The store brings together labels which wouldn't look out of place on a Gallagher brother: think Patagonia anoraks and Levi's 501's, topped off with a Polo Ralph Lauren bucket hat and Clarks desert boots. The store is something of a trailblazer too, sourcing exotic labels with simple, functional designs including French orthopaedic shoe retailer Anatomic and artsy smock label Arpenteur. In the window of the Soho store, which is decked out to look like a stock room, a poster simply reads: 'We sell good clothes'. They're not wrong.

—

1 Marshall Street, W1F 9BA.
020 7734 2585
www.oipolloi.com

SEE ALSO...

Folk (p13), Grenson (p15), Universal Works (p19), Oliver Spencer (p19), Content & Co (p22), Trunk (p31), Sefton (p41), Hub (p45), Article (p51), Hostem (p70), Sunspel (p73)

LASSCO

LASSCO – or, to give it its proper title, the London Architectural Salvage and Supply Co. – forms the backbone of Bermondsey's bustling Maltby Street Market. Marked by its glowing 'Aloha' entrance sign, this cavernous warehouse offers ample browsing opportunities, from coffee sack cushions to a magnificent assemblage of door knobs. Don't forget to check out the floors – LASSCO has been salvaging timber since the nineteenth century.

—

41 Maltby Street, SE1 3PA.
020 7394 8061
www.lassco.co.uk

VIVIEN OF HOLLOWAY

For those who wish they were born in a different era, Vivien of Holloway provides the perfect 1950s time warp. Vivien has been trading her rockabilly reproductions since the tender age of eighteen, and her Holloway Road pin-up parlour is filled with full-skirted froufrou frocks, wiggle skirts and pedal pushers. She also designs alternative bridal wear starting at just £89.

—

294 Holloway Road, N7 6NJ.
020 7609 8754
www.vivienofholloway.com

WHAT THE BUTLER WORE

Established in 1995, this ingeniously named shop has taken great care to maintain its reputation as one of the capital's most popular vintage shops. Specialising in fashion from the 1960s and 1970s, its hits include Mary Quant inspired minis and floral flares, while for the blokes there are psychedelic shirts and sharp Mad Men-style suits.

—

108 Lower Marsh, SE1 7AB.
020 7261 1968
www.whatthebutlerwore.co.uk

TOBIAS AND THE ANGEL

This charming shop in the heart of Barnes Village sports an unusual inventory of antiques, from oil can lamps to Staffordshire ceramics, and displays them in a cosy, uncontrived environment. Its own furniture range is made to measure from its workshop in Surrey, plus it's a dab hand at whipping up a scatter cushion or cat doorstop from its hand-block-printed fabric.

—

66 White Hart Lane, SW13 0PZ.
020 8878 8902
www.tobiasandtheangel.com

THE OLD CINEMA

Housed in a former Edwardian picture house, The Old Cinema is billed as London's only antique, vintage and retro department store. Attracting a high class of international interior scourers, the variety of treasures in this family-run emporium is ever changing and is particularly well-versed in kitting out home studies thanks to its wealth of Italian leather swivel chairs and mid-century desks.

—

160 Chiswick High Road, W4 1PR.
020 8995 4166
www.theoldcinema.co.uk

GONNERMANN

With a skew towards mid-century, Scandi-minimalist and industrial designs, this striking furniture shop in Highgate has been a favourite with interior designers and tastemakers since 1992. Founder Julian Gonnermann is an expert when it comes to retro Danish furniture for twenty-first-century homes, filling his shop with Grete Jalk sofas, Ole Wanscher armchairs and 1960s Teak sideboards.

—

408-410 Archway Road, N6 5AT.
07973 310 406
www.gonnermann.co.uk

◄ THE PEANUT VENDOR

Specialising in mid-century furniture that combines style and substance, The Peanut Vendor has grown from a tiny boutique to a sizeable store. Bauhaus and Hollywood Regency are among the key schools of design influence with Art Deco mirrors, G-Plan sideboards and French floor lamps, while little luxuries include great coffee at its in-store café.

—

6 Gunmakers Lane, Gunmakers Wharf, E3 5GG.
020 8981 8613
www.thepeanutvendor.co.uk

BLITZ

Choosing between vintage shops around Brick Lane is like trying to decide what to order at your favourite curry house. But Blitz is a contender for the top spot. Its sprawling two-storey warehouse may be daunting, but the layout is so easy to navigate even the laziest trawler will find the 1990s slip dress of their dreams. What's more, everything is cleaned before it hits the floor.

—

55-59 Hanbury Street, E1 5JP.
020 7377 0730
www.blitzlondon.co.uk

WILLIAM VINTAGE

Shopping at William Vintage is far from your average thrift shop rummage. William Banks-Blaney (aka the King of Vintage) has dressed a who's who of red carpet regulars, from Amal Clooney to Rihanna, from his vast collection of museum-worthy vintage pieces. Specialising in statement gowns and evening coats, Banks-Blaney believes that vintage looks its best when paired with modern-day accessories. Along with well-known fashion houses, from couture by Dior to Chanel tweed suits, his edit also champions lesser known names from bygone eras. Take William Travilla, who designed costumes for Marilyn Monroe including that iconic ivory dress, and Louis Feraud who was beloved by Brigitte Bardot. As such, you won't find any bargain bins here – typical buys can be anywhere in the region of £200 up to an eye-watering £25,000.

—

2 Marylebone Street, W1G 8JQ.
020 7487 4322
www.williamvintage.com

PELICANS & PARROTS

At number 40 Stoke Newington Road, collector of curiosities Juliet Da Silva stocks her shop with fine vintage threads sourced in Italy. A few doors up at number 81, her partner Ochuko Ojiro mans the homeware outpost – Pelicans & Parrots Black – which treasures stylish antique furniture and artefacts. Together, their taste for the weird and wonderful makes for one of Dalston's most eclectic shopping opportunities, whether you're after a 1980s Moschino jacket or a Bamileke wall hanging from Cameroon. If you fancy a Pina Colada after your perusing, the duo also run a subterranean rum shack called Below, which is hidden beneath its furniture shop – though you have to find it first. Tip: the secret door in the neighbouring Hang-Up Gallery might be a good place to start...

—

40 Stoke Newington Road, N16 7XJ.
020 3215 2083
www.pelicansandparrots.com

SEE ALSO...

Annie's (p36), The Restoration (p45), Strut (p45), Only Fools and Peacocks (p47), Circus (p52), Leftovers (p52), Woo Woo Boutique (p57), Threads (p63), Worn Not Torn (p65), B Southgate (p89), Found and Vision (p97), Rellik (p99), Phoenix on Golborne (p99), Jane Bourvis (p103), 88 Antiques (p103)

THE GOODHOOD STORE

East London brand Goodhood reinvents the
department store set-up for the Shoreditch
crowd. Everything it stocks – from sweatshirts
to tasteful smellies, stationery to stylish slippers
– showcases its knack for the niche. Once you're
done exploring every nook and cranny, the in-
store café is on hand with flat whites for
fatigued shoppers.

—

151 Curtain Road, EC2A 3QE.
020 7729 3600
www.goodhoodstore.com

A NEAT CONCEPT CONCEPT STORES

◀ DOVER ST MARKET

This ground-breaking retail playground is always full of surprises – the biggest of which came in 2016, when Dover Street Market relocated from its namesake street to the West End. The current DSM universe is roughly three times bigger and carries a wealth of achingly cool brands including Craig Green and Gosha Rubchinskiy, alongside an in-store bakery and ever-changing art installations.

—

18-22 Haymarket, SW1Y 4DG.
020 7518 0680
www.doverstreetmarket.com

ALEX EAGLE

Former fashion journalist turned design golden girl Alex Eagle is as sharp eyed as her name suggests and her Lexington Street address is in the little black book of every arbiter of taste in London. Cottage industry design collaborations and Picasso plates sit comfortably with clothes from the likes of Lemaire, Vita Kin and Eagle's own line of androgynous womenswear.

—

6-10 Lexington Street, W1F 0LB.
020 7589 0588
https://alexeagle.co.uk

UNTO THIS LAST

Tagged as a workshop in the city, this hyper-local homeware concept sits at the lesser-frequented tip of Brick Lane and is the hipster's answer to Ikea. Sort of. Its USP is simplistic furniture solutions with a Scandi flavour – the showroom is decked almost exclusively in plywood pieces with white laminate accents – and the opportunity to watch its skilled carpenters create them on site.

—

230 Brick Lane, E2 7EB.
0207 613 0882
unto-this-last.myshopify.com

◄ OTHER/SHOP

Offering an antidote to the big brand chains of neighbouring Oxford Street and Regent Street, Soho's OTHER/shop provides a platform for little known labels. Founded by former b Store directors Matthew Murphy and Kirk Beattie, here you will find wearable – but never generic – clothes from its own label as well as plimsolls by Stockholm's Eytys and playful knits by Peter Jensen. They also have excellent taste in potted plants.

—

21 Kingly Street, W1B 5QA.
020 7734 6846
www.other-shop.com

THE SHOP AT BLUEBIRD

This iconic West London hotspot is a favourite with the *Made in Chelsea* crowd. But don't hold that against it. A trip to Bluebird is rewarded with a sanctuary of well-considered pieces – from luxury labels to coffee table books – occupying an impressive 10,000-square-foot shop floor. Owners John and Belle Robinson (the brains behind British high street chain Jigsaw) also masterminded Mayfair's chic shopping hub Duke Street Emporium.

—

350 King's Road, SW3 5UU.
020 7351 3873
www.theshopatbluebird.com

MACHINE A

Run by Stavros Karelis and esteemed stylist Anna Trevelyan, Machine-A injects a jolt of creative energy into Soho's increasingly homogenised retail horizon. The crème de la crème of London's hot young fashion set – Christopher Shannon, Claire Barrow, Nasir Mazhar – find themselves in good company alongside insider heavyweights such as Raf Simons. But most exciting are the grassroots labels: Machine-A is not afraid to take a gamble on the next fresh-out-of-fashion-school star.

—

13 Brewer Street, W1F 0RH.
020 7734 4334
www.machine-a.com

SELFRIDGES

The great-grandfather of concept stores, Harry Gordon Selfridge's dream was to create a shop which was more than just a place where you could buy stuff, but where visitors could be entertained while they part with their hard earned cash. More than 100 years on and this iconic department store is still pushing the retail envelope. Recent attractions have included a carpark service station with cult handbag designer Anya Hindmarch, and a gender-neutral clothing floor.

—

400 Oxford Street, W1A 1AB.
0800 123 400
www.selfridges.com

LN-CC

There are few boutiques in London that command as much respect among fashion's inner circle as Late Night Chameleon Café. Having earned its reputation as a retail risk-taker with a sixth sense for the Next Big Thing, this exclusive place of brand worship requires you to book an appointment to walk its hallowed halls. Feel free to turn up on a whim, but there's no guarantee that someone will answer the doorbell.

—

18-24 Shacklewell Lane, E8 2EZ.
020 3174 0744
www.ln-cc.com

LUNA & CURIOUS

This independent shop on Shoreditch's cool Calvert Avenue was opened ten years ago by a collective of young artisans – ceramicists Polly George and Kaoru Parry and jeweller Rheanna Lingham. Their stock, which includes witty English teacups and beautiful feathered necklaces, take pride of place in their miniature department store, alongside a melting pot of fresh talent. Architectural hoops by minimalist jeweller Jenny Sweetnam, made in England bags from M.Hulot and lotions from social enterprise The Soap Co., which employs blind and disabled people in its East London workshop, are just a handful of the brands which have been lovingly sourced by the trio. The boutique also recently introduced its own line of knitwear and home accessories, which includes bright baby blankets and handmade scented candles. In essence, it's a gift-hunters dream.

24-26 Calvert Avenue, E2 7JP.
020 3222 0034
www.lunaandcurious.com

SEE ALSO...

The Monocle Shop (p32), Hexagone (p39), Search & Rescue (p47), Brixi (p52), Turpentine (p56), Joy (p57), Bias (p63), Modern Society (p72), By Walski (p73), Couverture & The Garbstore (p107)

STORM IN A TEACUP

With the aim of taking the 'fast' out of fashion, this Kingsland Road concept store champions a green approach to luxury clothing by buying and selling rare vintage. Stylist Joe Miller and model girlfriend Claudia Raba fill their boutique with pieces that have history sewn into every thread, from vintage Chanel handbags to Vivienne Westwood Pirate boots. There's also an old-fashioned sweet shop in store to sweeten the deal.

—

366 Kingsland Road, E8 4DA.
020 8127 5471
www.storminateacuplondon.com

LOWIE

Geared towards Herne Hill's yummy mummies, this eco-conscious boutique creates clothes with an easy wearability and minimal environmental impact. Ethically sourced cashmere sweaters and organic cotton sundresses are the brand's bread and butter and founder Bronwyn Lowenthal regularly visits her hand-selected manufacturers to ensure fair working conditions.

—

115 Dulwich Road, SE24 0NG.
020 7733 0040
www.ilovelowie.com

MINNA

Above a church on Brixton Road, you will find Minna Hepburn's eco-luxe vintage bridal boutique. Using antique lace and organic fabric to craft her gowns, the Finnish designer is as scrupulous about zero waste as she is bespoke design, employing the off-cuts for embellishments and accessories. In 2009 she launched a cute kidswear collection with each piece made entirely from end of roll textiles.

—

90 Brixton Road, SW9 6BE.
020 7735 3270
www.minna.co.uk

DANAQA

Danaqa means 'pleasantly surprised' in Amharic, which accurately sums up this humble shop in Notting Hill. Partners David and Nadia source unique items directly from women's groups across Africa and the Middle East, from beautiful Iranian embroidered jewellery to the handwoven Zambezi baskets. Amazingly, the pair can often recall the names of the women behind each creation.

—

Unit 21, 281 Portobello Road, W10 5TZ.
No phone.
www.danaqa.com

GANESHA

Trading in ethically-minded homeware for over 20 years, this fair trade boutique is one of the best loved in London. Sourcing goods from local co-operatives in India, Bangladesh and beyond, Ganesha's offering includes Bangali handloom bed linen, lamps made from recycled tin and leaf-wrapped organic soaps made in Pondicherry.

—

3-4 Gabriels Wharf, 56 Upper Ground, SE1 9PP.
020 7928 3444
www.ganesha.co.uk

THE THIRD ESTATE

Best known for its selection of vegan leather shoes, this popular Camden boutique has an emphasis on cruelty-free and ethically-traded fabric and manufacture. The Third Estate also champions socially-conscious brands including sweatshop-free denim label Monkee Genes and eco-fabric brand Komodo alongside its own printed t-shirt line, which fittingly uses organic inks.

—

27 Brecknock Road, N7 0BT.
020 3620 2361
www.thethirdestate.co.uk

TRAID DALSTON

Traid (which stands for Textile Recycling for Aid and International Development) is an initiative dedicated to stopping clothes from reaching landfills, with eleven charity shops across London. Unmistakable for its quirky window displays, Traid's latest outpost in Dalston is also the largest, stocking a wealth of pre-loved threads, homeware and haberdashery, plus its own waste textile fashion label Traidremade.

—

106-108 Kingsland High Street, E8 2NS.
020 7923 1396
www.traid.org.uk

◀ 69B BOUTIQUE

Situated amid the hustle and bustle of Broadway Market, this beautiful boutique shows just how far 'green' has come since the days of sludgy hemp. Owner Merryn Leslie – a talented stylist and former fashion editor at i-D Magazine – brings together some of the best labels with good intentions including Riyka, Beaumont Organic and East London label Here Today Here Tomorrow.

—

69B Broadway Market, E8 4PH.
020 7249 9655
www.69bboutique.com

URBAN OUTFITTERS

It may be one of the biggest names on the high street, but Urban Outfitters is ahead of the mass-produced-pack as far as sustainability is concerned. Its successful Urban Renewal range champions upcycled vintage, while its Oxford Street flagship has introduced an in-house brand Rework, which includes stylish, British-made collections crafted from remnant fabric.

—

200 Oxford Street, W1D 1NU.
020 7907 0800
www.urbanoutfitters.com

MARY'S LIVING & GIVING SHOP FOR SAVE THE CHILDREN

When retail doyenne Mary Portas opened her first charity shop for Save The Children in 2009, she single-handedly spearheaded a charity shop revolution. Now with eighteen shops in the capital, each with its own unique design, the community-based boutiques have built a reputation as the place to uncover luxury labels – often donated new by generous brands – at silly prices. The store in Chiswick, with its Jackson Pollock-style paint-splattered floor, is a good place to source works by local artists, while the picturesque Primrose Hill outpost is the best place to plunder cast-offs from the area's well-heeled residents. Victoria Beckham famously donated 25 of daughter Harper's outfits when the shop opened. Note: the best time to visit is late on Friday or first thing Saturday morning, when extra stock hits the floor in preparation for the weekend.

———

109 Regent's Park Road, NW1 8UR.
020 7586 9966
www.savethechildren.org.uk

SEE ALSO...

The People's Supermarket (p19), Family Tree (p23), The Keep Boutique (p57), NOM Living (p89), Goldfinger Factory (p102)

THE KIDS ARE ALRIGHT CHILDRENSWEAR & TOY SHOPS

◀ HONEYJAM

Dreamt up by lifelong friends Honey Bowdrey and Jasmine Guinness, Honeyjam is the sort of toyshop you wished you could have visited as a kid. Its line of traditional Merrythought teddy bears and wooden dollhouses may be among the most tasteful trinkets on offer, but the stash of cockroach catapults and fairy princess costumes show the pair know what kids today really want.

—

2 Blenheim Crescent, W11 1NN.
020 7243 0449
www.honeyjam.co.uk

GENTLY ELEPHANT

Just a stone's throw from the train station in South London's leafy Brockley you'll find Gently Elephant — a friendly neighbourhood kids clothing and gift shop populated with an expert selection of brands and a good supply of smiling staff. Among its most popular draws is a dedicated shoe wall lined with irresistible baby Birkenstocks and Pediped kicks.

—

169 Brockley Road, SE4 2RS.
020 8692 2881
www.gentlyelephant.co.uk

LITTLE GEMS

Hackney hipsters-in-the-making are all kitted out in clobber from this Victoria Park Village boutique. The stock of rompers and graphic tees are often locally-sourced, usually technicolour and always affordable. Owners and busy working mums Clair and Alex are keen purveyors of practicality with a dedication to barefoot shoe brands, a professional foot measuring service and in-store haircuts.

—

243 Victoria Park Road, E9 7HD.
020 8533 0006
www.littlegemsboutique.com

SEMMALINA

Journalist Sarah Standing and her friend Diana run Semmalina toy shop and, with seven children between them, are well informed when it comes to entertaining tots. The shop is transformed every few weeks so there's always something new to see and buy, but the bespoke party bag service and penny sweetshop are reasons alone to visit.

—

225 Ebury Street, SW1W 8UT.
020 7730 9333
No website.

◄ LA COQUETA

This adorable Spanish kidswear boutique in the Nappy Valley enclave of Hampstead stands out for its timeless, vintage-inspired designs and classic Iberian aesthetic. Catering to the under-7s, the shop's Peter Pan collar dresses and patent Mary Janes are a particular draw. Mercifully, there is also a play area at the back of the shop to keep wee ones busy while you browse.

—

5 Heath Street, NW3 6TP.
020 7435 1875
www.lacoquetakids.com

THE CROSS

One of the original – and still one of the best – independent lifestyle boutiques in London, this Holland Park gem boasts well-selected womenswear, eclectic homeware and great gifts. But this shop is as much about West London's smallest style set as is it their mums, with its hotchpotch of toy-box must-haves and mini-me pom-pom bags and breton tops.

—

141 Portland Road, W11 4LR.
020 7727 6760
www.thecrossshop.co.uk

MOLLY MEG

Stylish and cute meet in this design-led kids' store that does a fine line in printed fabric furnishings, from play mats to teepees. There's also a covetable collection of timeless playthings (crochet bunnies, wooden blocks and sequined fairy wings), contemporary furniture in miniature proportions and an array of bed linen in prints so cool you'll be left wishing they came in adult sizes.

—

111 Essex Road, N1 2SL.
020 7359 5655
www.mollymeg.com

EENYMEENY KIDS

After shutting the doors of its original Tufnell Park shop in 2015, cool kids' boutique Eenymeeny Kids is back and better than ever with a shiny new outpost on Fortess Road. Situated conveniently next door to ice-cream parlour Ruby Violet, this wonderful store is packed with unique toys and kidswear, from crochet music boxes to milk bottle print swaddle blankets.

—

116 Fortess Road, NW5 2HL.
020 3556 7472
www.eenymeenykids.co.uk

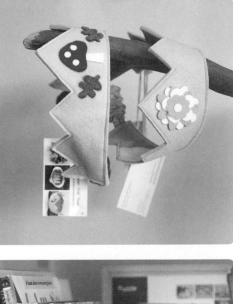

NIDDLE NODDLE

Is it a shop? Is it a playroom? Who cares, as long as the kids are happy. Aside from the big draws (namely the play kitchen and big yellow slide in the corner), Eilidh Fraser and Katrine Camillo also furnish Niddle Noddle with pocket money playthings, nostalgic wind-up toys and lovable clothing labels you won't find anywhere else.

—

5 Topsfield Parade, N8 8PR.
020 8347 4333
www.niddlenoddle.com

WILD & GORGEOUS

With two outposts in Primrose Hill and Notting Hill, Wild & Gorgeous has long been the go-to for West London's princesses to purchase their floaty frocks and heart-print faux fur coats. It's not short of famous fans either, having clothed the likes of Suri Cruise, Apple Martin and Harper Beckham, while sales spiked after David Cameron's daughters Nancy and Florence chose to wear floral dresses by the brand to bid goodbye to 10 Downing Street. The store has more recently branched out into boyswear and successfully doubled its appeal with cool polo knits, tailored joggers and camo-print jackets, filling a gap in the market for brilliant garb for boys.

—

73 Regent's Park Road, NW1 8UY.
020 7586 1552
www.wildandgorgeous.co.uk

SEE ALSO...

Olive Loves Alfie (p46), Dandy Star (p92), Bob & Blossom (p93), Caramel (p109), R.S. Currie & Co (p111), Fara Kids and Baby (p111)

FØREST LONDON

After the success of her ten-day pop up in 2010, Scandinavian design collector Eva Coppens set about to establish a permanent base, and Førest London was born. Mid-century Dutch and Swedish furniture by Arne Jacobsen, Hans Wegner and Børge Mogensen are among the vintage finds, while collaborations with contemporary artists gives shoppers fresh and affordable options.

—

115 Clerkenwell Road, EC1R 5BY.
020 7242 7370
www.forestlondon.com

LIBERTY

Venture past the signature silk scarves and new season It bags to the very top of this iconic department store to be rewarded with a warren of high-end homeware. Its famous haberdashery department is bursting with Liberty-print trimmings to transform your sewing box, or ascend to the quiet ceramics-filled rooms in the rafters and you may just have the place to yourself.

Regent Street, W1B 5AH.
020 7734 1234
www.libertylondon.com

PITFIELD LONDON

A trip to Pitfield is like visiting a globetrotting great-uncle – it's always on hand with a slab of cake and a haul of exotic treasures. Shaun Clarkson and Paul Brewster travel every month to fill their vast visual paradise with vintage crockery, Indian rugs and attention-grabbing kitchenware, while its spacious café provides a pit-stop while you ponder whether you need another Victorian jelly mould.

31-35 Pitfield Street, N1 6HB.
020 7490 6852
www.pitfieldlondon.com

JASPER MORRISON ▶

Influential industrial designer Jasper Morrison opened up shop within his office on Kingsland Road as 'an idealistic showroom'. And while everything in it is designed to put functionality ahead of aesthetics, that doesn't stop the space from being exceptionally beautiful. Everyday items from mostly anonymous designers are arranged in ever-changing and OCD-neat displays.

24B Kingsland Road, E2 8DA.
No phone.
www.jaspermorrisonshop.com

SCP EAST

Three decades since SCP first sprung up on Curtain Road, this interiors institution continues to deliver cutting-edge and creative homeware to East London's cool-hunters. Employing the talents of designers including Terence Woodgate and Konstantin Grcic, founder Sheridan Coakley has long established SCP East (and its sister store SCP West on Westbourne Grove) as pioneers in the furniture industry. Stylish, statement items are this store's raison d'être. Whether you're in the market for a new three-piece suite or a bath mat, each piece has been painstakingly selected for its modernist sensibility and compliment-attracting aesthetic. Head upstairs to browse the furniture, rugs and 'chair wall', while the ground floor is a haven of technology and contemporary lighting. It's particularly good to visit in September, when the store hosts international exhibitions during the London Design Festival.

—

135–139 Curtain Road, EC2A 3BX.
020 7739 1869
www.scp.co.uk

PETERSHAM NURSERIES ▶

Whether you've got a backyard or a window box, this glorious garden centre is a must-visit with more than just sacks of soils and potted nasturtiums on offer. Get lost in the greenery or pick up a planter for your green-fingered friend. Its restaurant and teahouse are also idyllic spots for a bit of posh nosh or a slice of cake.

—

Church Lane, Petersham Road, Richmond, TW10 7AB.
020 8940 5230
www.petershamnurseries.com

HOUSE OF HACKNEY

For those who crave a statement wall or a lamp shaped like a pineapple, your search ends with House of Hackney. Javvy M Royle and Frieda Gormley – partners in business and life – launched their brand in 2011 and their flagrant disregard for minimalism has resulted in a print-on-print-on-print approach. Head there for OTT wallpaper, a set of save-for-best guest towels or simply a good gawp.

—

131 Shoreditch High Street, E1 6JE.
020 7739 3901
www.houseofhackney.com

OLIVER BONAS

A high-end boutique with a strong high street presence, Oliver Bonas brings accessible luxury and a touch of chintzy kitsch to the homes of London's sensibly-heeled. With stores sprinkled across the capital and around the UK, High Street Kensington is home to its largest outpost and offers velvet chaise-lounges and patchwork cabinets alongside its cookbooks, scented candles and flamingo-print wrapping paper.

—

129 Kensington High Street, W8 6SU.
020 7937 4686
www.oliverbonas.com

THETHESTORE

Actress Meryl Fernandes (aka Afia Masood to Eastenders fans) found her footing in retail with Found, a vintage fashion shop on Hackney Road. After a quick renovation with the help of Swedish design brand Nonuform, she rechristened the space as thethestore, a lifestyle boutique full of things that she loves (and that you probably will too). The stark white shop is stocked with seemingly random objects, from Italian toothpaste to hand-thrown ceramics, but good design is the thread that unites them. There's also a good line of workwear-style separates by London based brand Otho and an impressive stack of niche magazines. One thing is certain, you may not know what you came in for but you won't leave empty handed.

—

205 Hackney Road, E2 8JL.
No phone.
www.thethestore.com

FUTURE AND FOUND

With a nostalgic take on thoroughly modern design, Future and Found offers Scandanavia-meets-Shoreditch homeware in the heart of North London's Tufnell Park. Housed in an old piano factory, owner Andrea Bates – who cut her design teeth as a buyer for Heals – chooses every item in the shop for its understated yet striking aesthetic. True to its name, stock includes pieces sourced from makers around the world and vintage treasures, alongside items from its own ever-expanding collection. Big ticket furniture items are quirky but not gimmicky, like the Eames rocking chair and horse-shaped wooden farm stool. Those with shallower pockets can brighten up their abode with a colourful coat rack or pair of geometric print tea towels. The spacious courtyard is home to plants and patio furniture, and houses a coffee hatch for a side of caffeine with your shop.

225A Brecknock Road, N19 5AA.
020 7267 4772
www.futureandfound.com

SEE ALSO...

Pentreath & Hall (p15), Thornback & Peel (p18), Botanique Workshop (p24), The Conran Shop (p33), Gill Wing Cookshop (p36), Aria (p39), Twentytwentyone (p40), Smug (p41), Adventures in Furniture (p41), Rouge (p46), Nook (p47), Prep Cook Shop (p47), Quaint & Belle (p65), Labour and Wait (p69), Elementary (p70), Monologue (p70), Klaus Haapaniemi (p73), Botany (p76), Triangle (p78), The Hackney Draper (p83), Everything But The Dog (p83), Two Columbia Road (p93), Native & Co (p110)

HOXTON STREET MONSTER SUPPLIES

Where else in London, or in the world for that matter, could you replenish your supply of cubed earwax (fudge) or fang floss (string)? This brilliantly bonkers boutique fills a gap in the market we never knew existed and donates its proceeds to the Ministry of Stories: an initiative set up by author Nick Hornby to help East London kids discover the magic of creative writing.

—

159 Hoxton Street, N1 6PJ.
020 7729 4159
www.monstersupplies.org

MUNGO & MAUD ▶

For pampered pugs and chichi chihuahuas, this Belgravia pet outfitters is the cat's whiskers. Since 2005, Mungo & Maud has been spoiling our four-legged friends with hand-stitched collars and homemade organic treats. Owners aren't left out either, with a selection of walking accoutrements including leather poop pouches and books such as 'Why Does My Cat Do That?'

—

79 Elizabeth Street, SW1W 9PJ.
020 7022 1207
www.mungoandmaud.com

KRISTINA RECORDS

Drawing in a high calibre of crate diggers from across London, this independent Dalston record shop is democratic in its music tastes, stocking brand new and old, mainstream and rare vinyl. Stock is all killer, no filler with underground sounds from cutting-edge synth and techno to long-forgotten gems from obscure disco and garage days.

—

44 Stoke Newington Road, N16 7XJ.
020 7254 2130
www.kristinarecords.com

HOP BURNS & BLACK

Jen and Glenn opened Hop Burns & Black to sell the three things they love most – craft beer, hot sauce and vintage vinyl. Turns out, the rest of London seems to share their enthusiasm. Sample a Kiwi coconut porter or the newest drop from Brockley Brewery on their drink-in tables, or take home a flagon of fresh beer and a bottle of Whitey's Bad Boy Jerk.

—

38 East Dulwich Road, SE22 9AX.
020 7450 0284
www.hopburnsblack.co.uk

◀ LINA STORES

When you can't make it to Puglia, there's Lina Stores. Serving Soho since 1944, this friendly, family-run Italian deli is the best place in the capital to stock up on burrata and biscotti. Work your way through the piles of panettone and hanging hams to the counter and be rewarded with fresh focaccia, fat olives, filled pasta and, of course, espresso.

—

18 Brewer Street, W1F 0SH.
020 7437 6482
www.linastores.co.uk

RACHEL VOSPER

This tiny boutique in Knightsbridge is home to Vosper's cult candles, available in thirteen signature scents. She will also fill a vessel of your choice, be it an antique tin or Branston Pickle jar, with perfumed beeswax charged by the gram. Plus, she is a font of knowledge when it comes to candle etiquette. Did you know that the ideal wick length is six millimetres?

—

69 Kinnerton Street, SW1X 8ED.
020 7235 9666
www.rachelvosper.com

ROULLIER WHITE

The back room in this unassuming shop in East Dulwich is home to the biggest selection of rare and unusual perfumes in the UK – none of which you will recognise, but all of which have the potential to become your new signature scent. The front showroom also stocks the full range of Mrs White's natural products: a cult line of old-school cleaning products and body lotions inspired by the owner's great grandmother's sworn-by recipes.

—

125 Lordship Lane, SE22 8HU.
020 8693 5150
www.roullierwhite.com

CLAPTON CRAFT

A vanguard in the craft beer revolution, this bottle shop in Lower Clapton is prized for its growlers – that's refillable bottles designed to keep draught beer fresh. Founders Will Jack and Tom McKim champion a range of bottled ales from local breweries including Beavertown, Five Points and Kernel, alongside regular European favourites such as Mikkeller. Two more outposts can be found in Kentish Town and Walthamstow.

—

97 Lower Clapton Road, E5 0NP.
020 3643 2669
www.claptoncraft.co.uk

PRESENT & CORRECT

Grown-up lovers of old school stationery will find much to line their pencil cases with at Present & Correct. This meticulously organised shop in Angel, founded by graphic designers Neal Whittington and Mark Smith in 2012, specialises in sourcing iconic and retro office supplies from Europe — some of them highly practical, others just aesthetically pleasing. Hermes baby typewriters sit side-by-side with calligraphy sets, old-fashioned airmail envelopes and vintage erasers, while the ingenious keyboard brush from Berlin is ideal for sweeping out even the most deeply embedded Hula Hoop crumbs. If you need any further encouragement to overhaul your workspace, the range of Bakelite desk tidies, big brass scissors and 1970s click calendars are also guaranteed to induce colleague envy.

—

23 Arlington Way, EC1R 1UY.
020 7278 2460
www.presentandcorrect.com

TOKYOBIKE

If you're the sort of cyclist who owns an Ally Capellino pannier and a Brooks leather saddle, chances are your two wheels of choice is a Tokyobike. This small, independent company, founded in the quiet suburb of Yanaka, set up shop in Shoreditch in 2012 and peddles simple, stylish bikes that are perfectly designed for inner city riding. They value comfort over speed and are light enough to carry up a flight of stairs, while the range of customisable frames, colours and accessories will appeal to those who like to get from A to B in style. They're reasonably priced too, starting at under £500. They offer a rental service available at just £12 per day, including a lock, lights and helmet. Also sharing retail space is Momosan Shop – a chic homeware store specialising in Japanese pottery.

87-89 Tabernacle Street, EC2A 4BA.
020 7251 6842
www.tokyobike.co.uk

SEE ALSO...

Borough Wines (p22), Brill (p23), Bagman & Robin (p25), McCaul Goldsmiths (p25), Cire Trudon (p31), Cass Art (p41), General Store (p60), Melange (p64), Flock & Herd (p65), Persepolis (p65), Mast Brothers (p73), Brahms & Liszt (p79), Lion Coffee + Records (p82), London Borough of Jam (p83), Choosing Keeping (p87), Harry Brand (p93), Nelly Duff (p93), Fez (p99), Honest Jon's (p103), Ally Capellino West (p103), Daylesford Notting Hill (p110)

ALFIES ANTIQUE MARKET

The capital's largest indoor antiques market is home to around 100 clued-up dealers, all of whom can give you a history lesson on the provenance of any item that may catch your eye. Opened in 1976 by Bennie Gray – who also owns Gray's Antiques in Mayfair – the former Art Deco department store now serves as a sprawling network of fine furniture and art split across four levels. You'll find early twentieth-century fashion and vintage trunks at Leslie Verrinder's Tin Tin Collectables on the first floor, and 1940s costume jewellery at Tony Durante, or seek out Dodo's around the corner for 1920s ad posters. Prices aren't throwaway, but neither is the stock – Alfies is a place for sourcing top tier antiques, not browsing ten-a-penny bric-a-brac. Plus there is ample opportunity to consider your investment over a cup of tea and slice of Victoria sponge at its humble rooftop café.

13-25 Church Street, NW8 8DT.
Open Tuesday–Saturday.
020 7723 6066
www.alfiesantiques.com

179

BROADWAY MARKET

Hackney residents with a taste for local produce make the weekly pilgrimage to Broadway Market to stock up on biodynamic wine and Violet bakery éclairs with a Climpson & Sons cold brew in hand. Neighbouring Netil Market on Westgate Street is also a hive for local designers on Saturday, with wares including hand-poured candles by Earl of East London.

—

Broadway Market, London E8 4QJ.
Open Saturday.
No phone.
www.broadwaymarket.co.uk

PORTOBELLO ROAD

This must-see on the tourist map is formed of many mini markets which span one long stretch of road. Start at Notting Hill Gate to browse silverware and antiques, travel further down to find food stalls before finishing with vintage fashion under the Westway flyover. Head out as early as the traders to beat the Saturday crowds, or visit on a Friday to source the best from emerging designers.

—

Portobello Road, W10 5TA.
Open Monday–Saturday.
020 7727 7684
www.portobelloroad.co.uk

CAMDEN MARKET

Camden's colourful collection of markets are as eclectic as the characters that stalk them. The market proper (on the Buck Street junction) is a busy jumble of club wear and graphic t-shirts; Stables Market offers vintage fashion bolt holes; while the pretty riverside Camden Lock provides everything from home furnishings to cool kidswear. Be ready to join the rabble if you venture there on a Saturday.

—

Camden Lock Place, NW1 8AF.
Open daily.
020 3763 9900
www.camdenmarket.com

WEST NORWOOD FEAST

This neighbourhood market-cum-social enterprise is powered by volunteers and was launched to give SE27 a boost. It is spread across several sites: exit West Norwood station to find Retro Village's vintage fashion and furnishings, keep walking to the kid-centric Family Hub, get some grub at the high street Food Fair, before reaching the crafty Artisans' Market on Norwood Road.

—

Norwood Road, SE27 0HS.
Open the first Sunday of every month.
No phone.
www.westnorwoodfeast.com

SPITALFIELDS

This East End stalwart – once a Sunday special, now a seven-day operation – centres on a different theme each day, from antiques on a Thursday to a retro extravaganza on Saturdays. The vibrant weekend Backyard Market and the Sunday UpMarket are close by on Brick Lane's Truman Brewery. Note: Queues for the ATM are long, but worth the wait for the cockney translation.

—

Brushfield Street, E1 6AA.
Open daily.
020 7377 1496
www.spitalfields.co.uk

BOROUGH MARKET

London's most famous foodie thoroughfare is also the oldest, celebrating its millennial year in 2014. It is the busiest too, with street food vendors and stalls piled high with rare-breed meat, artisanal cheese and seasonal veg, all bringing in a constant stream of shoppers on the hunt for a gastronomic adventure. Arrive early and bring your appetite.

—

8 Southwark Street, SE1 1TL.
Open Monday–Saturday.
020 7407 1002
www.boroughmarket.org.uk

MALTBY STREET MARKET

Along with a tasty cache of street food vendors, this bustling weekend market is also home to the Little Bird Gin bar and St John Bakery who have settled in under its railway arches. Follow the tracks down to nearby Spa Terminus to find producers including The Kernel Brewery and Mons Cheese who open up their workshops to shoppers on Saturdays.

Ropewalk, SE1 3PA.
Open Saturday–Sunday.
No phone.
www.maltby.st

◄ BOXPARK

This modern mall constructed from shipping containers landed underneath Shoreditch High Street underground station in 2011 and boasts an ever-changing roster of compact concessions. Current favourites include cool clogs from Swedish Hasbeens, minimalist Scandi jewels at Pärla and rustic tableware by Decorum. Cult makeup bag swag is also up for grabs at BeautyMART, while the steady-handed staff at Imarni Nails will deliver killer nail art in no time. It caters to hunger pangs too, since the top deck is home to a wealth of tasty treats and tipples, from Cotton's Rhum Shack and Falafelicious, to Dalston's pizza-by-the-slice emporium Voodoo Ray. Boxpark also has a second site that holds bragging rights to 42 bars and restaurants in Croydon's formerly derelict Ruskin Square.

—

2–10 Bethnal Green Road, E1 6GY.
Open daily.
020 7033 2899
www.boxpark.co.uk

GREENWICH MARKET

The first thing that hits you upon entering Greenwich Market is the aroma, as spicy Punjabi curries jostle for airtime with fryer-fresh chips and sexed-up burgers. But this compact covered market is a treat for the eyes too, with its World Heritage Site surroundings and crafty paraphernalia. Browse the assorted knick-knacks before checking out the Cutty Sark or heading to the Meantime Brewery for a patriotic pale ale.

—

5B Greenwich Market, SE10 9HZ.
Open daily.
020 8269 5096
www.greenwichmarketlondon.com

SEE ALSO...
Cabbages & Frocks market (p33), Clerkenwell Vintage Fashion Fair (p25)

◀ PAXTON AND WHITFIELD

Original purveyors of fine English cheeses, Paxton & Whitfield have been in business for over 200 years. In 1850, they were appointed the official cheesemonger to Queen Victoria and still hold Royal Warrants of Appointment to Queen Elizabeth II and The Prince of Wales. Sample the Wild Garlic Cornish Yarg or the Oxford Isis washed in honey mead and expect to queue for your Stilton at Christmas.

---

93 Jermyn Street, SW1Y 6JE.
020 7930 025
www.paxtonandwhitfield.co.uk

JJ FOX

The tobacconist of choice for the likes of Winston Churchill and Oscar Wilde, this prestigious cigar merchant has been trading since 1787. Inside you will find a walk-in humidor featuring Havana's finest, plus a diminutive museum displaying memorabilia charting its legacy. It is also one of the few places left in London where you can legally smoke indoors – purely to sample the goods, of course.

---

19 St James's Street, SW1A 1ES.
020 7930 3787
www.jjfox.co.uk

L. CORNELISSEN & SON

Whether you're the next Van Gogh or just a devoted doodler, this legendary art store can't fail to leave you inspired. Supplying the capital's painters since 1855, L. Cornelissen & Son wears its years well with its bottle-green shop front, ceiling-high shelves crammed with jars of bright pigment and potfuls of charm.

---

105 Great Russell Street, WC1B 3RY.
020 7636 1045
www.cornelissen.com

HORNETS

This gentleman's outfitters sports a fine pedigree of second-hand and specialist attire – most of it tweed. Its Lilliputian emporium on Kensington Church Walk (opposite the former home of Ezra Pound), is the oldest men's vintage clothing shop in the country, with formalwear and Fedoras, waistcoats and winklepickers in good supply.

---

2 Kensington Church Walk, W8 4NB.
020 7937 2627
www.hornetskensington.co.uk

JAMES SMITH & SONS LTD

Established in 1830, this world-famous family-run brolly boutique has been keeping Londoners dry since the Victorian era. Its visually stunning premises on New Oxford Street is the first name in rainy day accessories – some finished with intricately-wrought handles and silverware, others boasting modern folding techniques – as well as walking sticks, cut to length while you wait.

—

Hazelwood House, 53 New Oxford Street, WC1A 1BL.
020 7836 4731
www.james-smith.co.uk

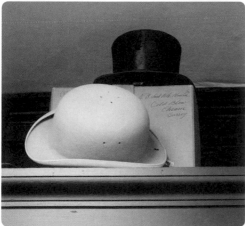

LOCK & CO

Widely accredited as 'the best hatters in the world' (legend has it that a postcard was delivered to the shop addressed as such), Lock & Co have been making fine English hats since 1676. Admiral Lord Nelson and Winston Churchill were among its distinguished customers. It is also famed for creating the distinctive domed Coke hat – more commonly known as the bowler – immortalised by Charlie Chaplin.

—

6 St James's Street, SW1A 1EF.
020 7930 8874
www.lockhatters.co.uk

DR HARRIS & CO

London may be a very different place to what it was in 1790, but reassuringly little has changed at Dr Harris & Co. Aside from the location (its original home was down the road at number 11), the old English apothecary continues to supply St James's most discerning with soaps, shaving brushes and skincare from its original medicine cabinets.

—

29 St James's Street, SW1A 1HB.
020 7930 3915
www.drharris.co.uk

◀ FLORIS

There are few shops as fragrant as Floris, or with quite as impressive a legacy. Since it was founded in 1730, Floris's fine perfumes and toiletries have been treasured by King George IV, Florence Nightingale and Marilyn Monroe. In 1989, its factory in Devon was opened by Princess Diana and its fine products continue to be made there as well as in the perfumery behind its founding shop.

—

89 Jermyn Street, SW1Y 6JH.
020 7747 3612
www.florislondon.com

THE BUTTON QUEEN

Polished to plastic, big to small, old to new, The Button Queen boasts more buttons than the pearliest of kings. Just a few metres from V V Rouleaux (see page 193), this long-established retailer's fascination with the humble fastening spans glass, enamel, horn and silver, while services include sourcing replacement buttons, button recovering and bespoke button dyeing.

—

76 Marylebone Lane, W1U 2PR.
020 7935 1505
www.thebuttonqueen.co.uk

V V ROLEAUX

Keeping craft traditions thriving in the capital, florist turned haberdasher Annabel Lewis's well-loved shop is a wonderland of rainbow ribbons and all the trimmings. A utopia for designers and decorators, past customers include Tom Ford and Manolo Blahnik, while V V Rouleaux also supplied the Duchess of Cambridge with silk-satin cream ribbon for her bridesmaid dresses.

—

102 Marylebone Lane, W1U 2QD.
020 7224 5179
www.vvrouleaux.com

SEE ALSO...
Connock & Lockie (p19), Cadenhead's Whisky Shop & Tasting Room (p29), Angela Flanders (p86)

SCHOOL OF LIFE

A brand 'devoted to developing emotional intelligence', the School of Life stocks books with titles such as *How To Stay Sane* and *How To Change The World*. Its shop in Bloomsbury is also home to card games to help you find your ideal partner, career crisis prompt cards and scented candles designed to invoke Plato's concept of utopia.

—

70 Marchmont Street, WC1N 1AB.
020 7833 1010
www.theschooloflife.com

CLAIRE DE ROUEN BOOKS

With tomes including works by David Bailey, Nick Knight and Diane Arbus, this tiny bookshop – established above a sex shop on Charing Cross Road in 2005 – is always swarming with fashion students and photography buffs. While its owner Claire sadly passed away in 2012, Royal College of Art-trained painter Lucy Moore continues to lead a new chapter for this Soho icon.

—

125 Charing Cross Road, WC2H 0EW.
020 7287 1813
clairederouenbooks.com

SKOOB

This first-rate second-hand bookshop recycles knowledge on a vast number of subjects, from philosophy, maths and science to art, literature and politics. Its spacious shop in the Brunswick Centre is crammed with over 55,000 titles and, unlike its name, the service isn't backwards. The personable staff can help you locate a proverbial needle in a literary haystack.

—

66 The Brunswick, Marchmont Street, WC1N 1AE.
020 7278 8760
www.skoob.com

STANFORDS

Since 1901, Covent Garden's famous map and travel bookshop has helped the likes of Ernest Shacklewell and Florence Nightingale, as well as mere mortals from across the globe, find their way. Don't miss the giant A to Z map of London in the basement, the room full of globes or its new café decorated with historic maps from the Edward Stanford Cartographic Collection.

—

12-14 Long Acre, WC2E 9LP.
020 7836 1321
www.stanfords.co.uk

FOSTERS BOOKSHOP

This Chiswick bookshop has been in owner Stephen Foster's family for over 45 years and specialises in antiquarian books and rare first editions. Stephen also enjoys a second career in film and has stocked the shelves of fictional characters including James Bond and Sherlock Holmes with topical and period-accurate publications.

—

183 Chiswick High Road, W4 2DR.
020 8995 2768
www.fostersbookshop.co.uk

LIBRERIA

As bookshops around the country collapse, this shiny new shrine to the written word stands in defiance of the recession. Conceived by Second Home's founders Rohan Silva and Sam Aldenton – a buzzing co-working space located next door – this bright yellow bastion of bookselling places its spotlight firmly on cutting-edge independent publishers. Its stock is arranged not in alphabetical order or by standard genres, but by subjects such as 'Family', 'Love' and 'Enchantment for the Disenchanted', while guest curators including award-winning writer Jeanette Winterson and founder of *New York Review Books* Edwin Frank will select shelves of their favourite titles. There is also a strict no-phones policy to save you from any digital distractions, while its bookbinding workshops and basement printing press serves to cement its dedication to creating and preserving literature in its physical form.

—

65 Hanbury Street, E1 5JP.
No phone.
www.libreria.io

◄ MAISON ASSOULINE

This cathedral of culture from luxury French publishing empire Assouline is part bookstore, part museum, part plush cocktail bar. Browse their extensive coffee table books on fashion, art and architecture, sip champagne in the Swans Bar or ascend the grand staircase in the former banking hall to lose yourself in rooms devoted to quiet contemplation and cabinets of curiosities.

—

196A Piccadilly, W1J 9DY.
020 3327 9370
www.assouline.com

ARTWORDS BOOKSHOP

With two outposts populating artist-dense areas (Hoxton's Rivington Street and Broadway Market in London Fields), Artwords and its collection of contemporary visual publications are well positioned. Head there to brush up on your knowledge of fine art, photography and graphic design or browse its comprehensive range of international industry magazines.

—

69 Rivington Street, EC2A 3AY.
020 7729 2000
www.artwords.co.uk

LUTYENS & RUBINSTEIN

Literary agents Sarah Lutyens and Felicity Rubinstein opened a shop in 2009 with the aim of selling only books that they loved to read. To this day, their excellent literary taste and devotion to selecting titles that come with a personal endorsement has led to Lutyens & Rubinstein becoming a much-loved landmark in Notting Hill. It is also for this reason that you will find all manner of narrative in their light-filled shop, from fiction and non-fiction to children's books, poetry and art, as well as a section dedicated to their all-time favourite reads. Naturally, staff members are brilliant at recommendations. It is also home to a selection of equally idiosyncratic extras, including paperweights, reading glasses, illustrations by Hugo Guinness and homemade preserves.

—

21 Kensington Park Road, W11 2EU.
020 7229 1010
www.lutyensrubinstein.co.uk

GOSH! COMICS

A little comic shop with a reputation that dwarfs its size, Gosh! has brought fans of capes and kapows together for 25 years. Its range of graphic novels is second to none and encompasses the standard superhero stuff through to cult manga and original underground artwork. There is no better place in London to get your geek on.

—

1 Berwick Street, W1F 0DR.
020 7636 1011
www.goshlondon.com

SEE ALSO...

Review (p62), Books for Cooks (p108), Persephone Books (p16), Bookends (p25), Daunt Books (p33), Bookmongers (p57), Pages of Hackney (p83)

INDEX

Quarto is the authority on a wide range of topics.

Quarto educates, entertains and enriches the lives of
our readers – enthusiasts and lovers of hands-on living.

www.QuartoKnows.com